P9-CEY-026

Terrariums & Miniature Gardens

By the Editors of Sunset Books and Sunset Magazine

LANE BOOKS · MENLO PARK, CALIFORNIA

Edited by Kathryn Arthurs

Design: John Flack

Illustrations: Bettina Borer

COVER: Miniature garden contains (see diagram):
(A) *Chamaedorea elegans;* (B) *Asparagus setaceus;*
(C) *Maranta leuconeura;* (D) *Selaginella;* (E) *Pilea depressa;*
(F) *Fittonia verschaffeltii;* (G) *Pilea cadierei.*
Garden was planted by Ah Sam Nursery,
San Mateo, California. Photographed by George Selland, Moss Photography.

Executive Editor, Sunset Books: David E. Clark

Seventh Printing April 1974

Copyright © Lane Magazine & Book Company, Menlo Park, California. First Edition 1973. World rights reserved. No part of this publication may be reproduced by any mechanical, photographic, or electronic process, or in the form of a phonographic recording, nor may it be stored in a retrieval system, transmitted, or otherwise copied for public or private use without prior written permission from the publisher. Library of Congress No. 72-92519. Title No. 376-03781-4. Lithographed in the United States.

Contents

LEADED glass containers (above) are decorated with stained glass patterns. Lid on large terrarium makes it accessible. Green-tinted glass on 5-gallon demi-john (right) requires plants with bold leaf forms.

Terrariums

Terrariums provide a unique method of indoor gardening enabling both the seasoned green thumber and the novice to enjoy nature's greenery in a capsulated form. Landscaped and scaled to the size of the container, the garden is encased in glass or plastic. A terrarium controls its own atmosphere, sustains a rain cycle, and stabilizes interior temperatures. Its isolation inside the container, coupled with the use of sterilized soil and pest-free nursery plants, keeps pest or disease attacks to a minimum. Like an incubator, a terrarium with its ideal conditions protects its contents from the outside world.

The limited amount of space allows landscaping only on a Lilliputian scale. But you apply the same principles as for full-scale, outdoor garden landscaping: vary plants by height, shape, leaf structure, and color. Individual plants should blend into the total picture, not upset it; choose plants for their effectiveness in the grouping as well as for their individual qualities.

A terrarium garden is unique in controlling its atmosphere. A high level of humidity, necessary for many plants, is maintained. The rain cycle keeps moisture at a constant level. Interior temperatures are stabilized by the container which separates the plants from fluctuating exterior conditions. Unless already present when planting takes place, diseases and pests find it hard to enter the isolated garden.

The perfect growing conditions a terrarium offers, as well as its unusual appeal, makes it a popular form of gardening for the beginner, and its versatility (it can be a seedling bed or a hospital for ailing plants) endears it to the horticulturally sophisticated.

This book defines a terrarium as a covered, enclosed miniature garden. Open gardens, such as those planted in brandy snifters or open globes, technically become terrariums only if covered with some type of lid. Open or semi-open containers cannot retain humidity, require more frequent watering, are more vulnerable to attacks from pests or diseases, and allow temperature fluctuation. They do, however, permit planting a wider selection of plants, for many plants do not need the high humidity levels found in a terrarium. Most succulents and cacti, for example, cannot tolerate terrarium conditions. Open and semi-open container gardens are discussed in Chapter 2, "Miniature Gardens." A wide selection of plants suitable for planting in terrariums and/or miniature gardens are described and explained in Chapter 3, the "Plant Selection Guide." Many of these plants are pictured as well.

Because terrarium gardens are such a novelty and tend to arouse viewers' curiosities, be prepared to answer questions such as, "How did the plants get in there?" and, "Why do the plants survive?" The "how" is fully explained in the section on terrarium planting, pages 12-22. The "why" is more complex; the following section offers a simplified version of the manner in which basic plant needs are fulfilled inside a closed terrarium container.

UNDERSTANDING PLANT PROCESSES

Two interdependent processes, photosynthesis and respiration, take place throughout the life of a plant. The products created during one process are used in the cycle of the other process.

THE FIRST TERRARIUM

Over 100 years ago, the accidental sprouting of a fern led to the terrarium idea.

Dr. Nathaniel B. Ward, an English surgeon who was also a natural history hobbyist, found that he was unable to grow the bog ferns he wanted in his London garden. He blamed this failure on quantities of factory smoke in the air.

Some time later, he was experimenting with the chrysalis of a sphinx moth that he had buried in moist earth and placed in a bottle. In a few weeks, he noticed that a fern and a grass seedling had sprouted in the bottle. He was astounded to find the same fern that had failed to live in his own garden was flourishing.

Dr. Ward was so intrigued that he experimented with other plants in different kinds of covered containers. He found if plants had light, still air, humidity, and even moisture they could thrive for years without care or fresh water.

Following the publication of his findings, the popularity of covered glass gardens grew rapidly. Known as Wardian Cases, they were constructed in a wide variety of shapes and sizes. Contemporary Victorians described them as "elegant and pleasing additions to the most tasteful and elaborately furnished drawing room."

But the idea of the Wardian Case had a practical side as well. Plants that previously were unable to survive long ocean voyages could now be shipped to distant ports. When they were sealed in these cases, extreme temperature changes, wind, sea air, and lack of care did not affect even the most exotic and delicate plant.

As a result of the Wardian Cases, new plant-based industries were created. The establishment of the entire tea industry in India succeeded because plants could now be shipped from Shanghai. Rubber trees were successfully transported from Brazil to Ceylon.

These plant exchanges were not limited only to agriculture. Botanical gardens were now able to receive exotic and rare plants from all over the world. Many of the garden plants we routinely grow and enjoy are available due to Dr. Ward's discovery.

Present day adaptations of Wardian Cases find enclosed gardens in cider jugs, wine bottles, tank aquariums, and plexiglas cubes. Contemporary craftsmen are creating unusual containers constructed of stained glass, leaded glass, wood and glass combinations, even plastic.

Dr. Ward's century-old discovery has been expanded and changed into the terrariums that we plant and enjoy today—all because of a moth.

The Ecologic Interaction of Plant Processes

Photosynthesis is the process by which plants manufacture their own food. They take in energy from the sun or light source, carbon dioxide from the air, and water from the soil; then these items are combined to create plant sugars. Plant sugars are a versatile food: they can supply energy to the plant immediately, be stored as food for later use, or be used as building material within the plant body. Nutrients taken in from the soil help in the production of these plant sugars, as well as in the growth of the plant.

While photosynthesis is at work, another process called respiration is taking place. The plant sugars are "burned" to provide energy for all plant functions. Every portion of the plant—from the topmost leaves to the bottom roots—requires its share of energy to sustain it.

Inside a terrarium, these processes are confined to a small, self-contained area. For the photosynthetic process, the sun or other light source provides the

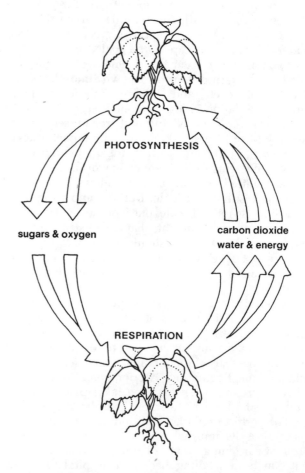

TOP plant represents photosynthesis; bottom plant, respiration. Arrows show product interaction.

energy, carbon dioxide is taken from the air in the container, and moisture is constantly being replenished by the rain cycle (see diagram, at right). Since slow plant growth is desired in the contained garden, the limited amount of nutrients present in the soil layer is sufficient.

For respiration, the plant sugar created by photosynthesis is burned for energy to carry on necessary plant functions, oxygen is taken from the air, and carbon dioxide is produced and recycled back to the atmosphere for use in the photosynthetic process. Oxygen is recycled by evaporation. The diagram shows the interaction of the various elements.

The terrarium garden is a conservationist's dream, for it efficiently uses and reuses the various elements present to fulfill its needs. A closer study of the give-and-take relationship between a plant and its terrarium environment might help us in the larger task of conserving and recycling the various elements present on our earth. Ecologists take note!

The Rain Cycle

Once sufficient moisture is introduced into a closed terrarium, a rain cycle is established. Moisture is taken into the plant through the root system, passes through the leaves by transpiration (the process in which water vapor is given off from leaf surfaces), then evaporates into the air. Since the limited atmosphere cannot absorb this excess moisture, the moisture is condensed on the container sides, "fogging" the glass or plastic. When the moisture builds up, it behaves like minute clouds, "raining" the moisture back into the soil layer. This process is continually repeating itself.

This cycle not only provides the garden with constant moisture, it also frees the indoor gardener from daily checks for moisture and bi-weekly waterings. As long as condensation is present on the container sides, sufficient moisture is present. If not, it's time to rewater.

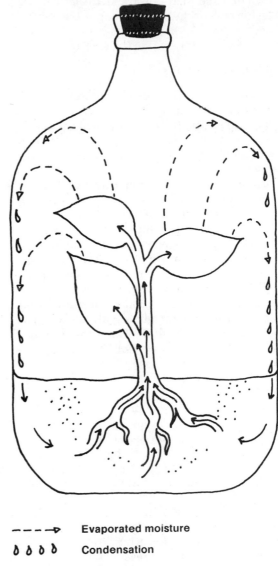

- - - →   **Evaporated moisture**

᠔ ᠔ ᠔ ᠔   **Condensation**

——→   **Moisture**

ARROWS follow the Rain Cycle process: from moisture in ground to water vapor in air back to moisture.

PLANNING THE TERRARIUM

Before delving headlong into planting a terrarium, a few preliminary decisions need to be considered. Consider these questions together, for each decision will affect the other two:

- Where will the garden be displayed?
- What type of container will accent the room and the garden to the best advantage?
- How many and what type of plants will be included?

Plant selection should be determined by the size of the container and the light available in the chosen location. Location depends on the available light and the appropriateness of a miniature garden as a room accent. Containers should be selected by their shape and design for a given location and the number and size of plants to be included. This interaction between container, plants, and location will determine if the terrarium is merely a contained garden set in a room or a decorating accent that arouses curiosity and creates a point of interest in the room.

Another important element to be considered at this time is the soil layer. Although soil is not a major design decision, it is vital to a thriving terrarium and requires advance planning. A special section (pages 11-12) explains the various soil elements to be included and their purpose in the garden. Instructions for preparing your own potting mix are included.

Finding a Location

Like a painting or a piece of sculpture, a terrarium adds an artistic touch to any room. Use one where both the room and the terrarium will be displayed to their best advantage. Then be prepared for the deluge of questions—a terrarium is a sure-fire conversation piece.

In choosing the location consider the garden's requirements as well as the surrounding decor. The basic needs of a terrarium are few: sufficient light and controlled temperature. Once a location meets these requirements, give your green thumb free rein.

Plants have varying light requirements—one point to consider when choosing terrarium cohabitants. The location chosen for your garden should provide enough light to sustain good plant growth and supply enough energy for photosynthesis (see page 6). (Light requirements of plants are listed in the Plant Selection Guide, pages 44-79.) Flowering plants and plants with variegated foliage require more light than other foliage plants.

Diffused light, not direct sunlight, is recommended for enclosed gardens. (Diffused light is defined as light coming through a lightweight window curtain. A north window will also provide light but no direct sun.) The disadvantage of direct sunlight is that it is magnified as it passes through a glass container, raising the interior temperature and scorching plants.

If the best location in a room is a dark corner, there are alternatives: artificial light can be provided (see page 39) or the terrarium can be moved daily to a well-lit spot for a reasonable length of time (approximately 10-12 hours).

The second requirement in choosing a location is correct temperature. Though many plants prefer cooler temperatures than people, plants tend to adapt easily to a normally heated house. But they will not tolerate drastic temperature changes or drafts, two problems eliminated by terrariums. The contained atmosphere keeps the interior temperature constant, and the glass or plastic walls exclude drafts. Do not place a terrarium over or near a heat source, however; the interior temperature can rise to stifling heights in a very short time.

A terrarium or bottles planted with alpine or woodland plants is an exception to the constant temperature rule. These plants thrive on warmish days and cool nights. If you wish to sustain them for any period of time, it is best to put them in a cool spot at night to help simulate their natural habitat. This can be in an unheated garage, storage room, or outside if there is no danger of freezing.

Choosing a Container

When selecting a terrarium container, let your imagination roam at will. A container candidate is one that can hold enough soil to support plant life, is made of clear or lightly tinted glass or other transparent material, and can be covered easily to create a humid atmosphere. Size will be determined by the planned location and the plants to be included.

Department stores, grocery stores, gift shops, hardware stores, and antique stores, as well as nurseries and garden supply stores, become treasure troves for the terrarium planter. The most common terrariums are planted in open globes, brandy snifters, and discarded fish bowls and aquarium tanks; all are readily available in varying sizes. (Remember to provide a cover for any open container.) Bottle gardens are usually seen in cider jugs and half-gallon wine bottles.

But don't let these easily obtainable containers limit your thinking. Use your ingenuity. Glass canisters, display domes, decanters, antique (and reproduction) fruit jars and medicine bottles are all possibilities. So are any other unique containers that meet the requirements. The more unusual the container is, the more intriguing the terrarium will be. A collection of both common and uncommon container possibilities is shown on page 9.

Humidity is the key to a thriving terrarium garden. A lid or covering conserves this humid atmosphere by retaining the moisture present in the container (see The Rain Cycle, page 7). If your container does not have a lid, improvise. A pane of glass cut proportionally to cover the opening will work well and not detract visually. Plastic kitchen wrap stretched over the opening will also trap the moisture but is less attractive. Airtight coverings can be removed periodically to allow fresh air circulation. A bottle garden does not require a cover, for very little moisture can evaporate through the narrow opening.

If the container you've selected is constructed of lightly tinted glass, choose shade loving plants. The Plant Selection Guide, pages 44-79, lists the varying light preferences of plants. Because tinted glass tends to obscure the view, choose plants with bold leaves or interestingly marked foliage. Since tinted glass allows less light to pass through, providing a well-lighted location is even more important.

Any container that meets the necessary requirements of size, transparency, and ability to retain humidity can be used as a terrarium to accent any room or decor. Although a roomful of period furniture might look best with an antique container of the same era, almost any container can blend nicely into the room. The container itself—though initially eye-catching—is secondary; the real focal point will be the miniature garden viewed through glass.

COLLECTION OF CONTAINERS. *Top row, from left to right: plexiglas cube; reproduction fruit jar; clear glass wine bottle; antique medicine bottle; clear glass canister. Second row: cider jug; large sized brandy snifter; cracker jar with metal lid; tinted wine bottle; open globe. Bottom row: reshaped, 5-gallon water bottle; aquarium; 5-gallon water bottle.*

CHOOSING plants in proportion to container size is easy if you take the container along when you shop.

BEFORE planting, establish the landscape. Arrange plants in nursery pots to find a pleasing design.

Selecting the Plants

To become part of a thriving garden, terrarium plants need more than exotic names or an unusual appearance; they must be compatible with each other and their environment. Choose plants that prefer the high humidity, moist soil, constant temperature, and low light intensity that a terrarium offers. A slow growth pattern is another desirable characteristic for terrarium plants. Any plant that meets these requirements can fill a spot in your landscape plan.

The number of plants to be included will depend on the size of the container. All terrariums should contain a variety of tall plants, medium-sized plants, and ground covers. Take the container to the nursery when you shop for plants. Estimating the number of plants and their sizes in relation to it at this time will avoid extensive pruning or another quick trip to a nursery before the container can be planted.

An interesting outdoor landscape contains a wide variety of plants; apply this same principle to a terrarium garden. Vary the plants by height, shape, color of foliage, and bold or delicate leaf forms. While all the plants are still in nursery pots, single out a dominant plant to be the focal point, usually a tall plant with bold or variegated leaves, arranging the other plants around it. Planning the arrangement before planting (as shown in the picture above right) gives a basic idea of how the garden will appear. Keep in mind that most terrariums will be viewed— and should be interesting—from all sides, even from the top.

If you want to protect your garden from disease or pests, quarantine plants before planting them in a terrarium. Two effective methods of quarantine are to place a bell dome over the plant in the clay pot (see page 26) or to transplant the plant into a chemist's flask or glass jar. Both methods simulate the ideal conditions of a terrarium. Allow plants to stay in the isolated environment for 2-3 weeks. A diseased plant or a pest infestation should surface in this length of time.

These same methods of quarantine are also useful in determining whether a particular plant can adjust to terrarium life. If you have a plant you'd like to try in a terrarium but can find no information about its requirements, quarantine it. If it survives for 3-4 weeks, it can be used to accent the landscape.

Don't mix backyard plants with those from nurseries or hothouses. Backyard plants are hardy and live in an environment where nature tends to keep pests in check through predators or competitors. But they may bring pests into the sheltered world of the terrarium and cause damage to the rest of its plants.

The Plant Selection Guide, pages 44-79, lists individual plant requirements and indicates possible terrarium companions. Study this guide and be familiar with plants you want before purchasing them; an educated buyer saves much time and effort.

Adding Accents

Just as statuary, bird baths, and sundials promote the feeling of nature in outdoor gardens, a similar accent can benefit a terrarium. Follow nature's example; decorate with understatement. A tiny stick covered with moss or lichen, a border of tiny, polished pebbles, or a piece of lava rock riddled with indentations provides subtle interest without distracting from the garden itself. Other possibilities are snail or seashells sans former inhabitants, interesting pieces of driftwood, small pine cones or seed pods, and gnarled pieces of bark.

Use ceramic figurines and artificial or dried flowers and foliage with caution. Figures that resemble those in nature, such as ceramic mushrooms, frogs, or snails, at least suggest a natural setting. Beware of artificial additions that are garishly colored and stick out like the proverbial sore thumb. A dash of whimsy is fine as long as it blends quietly into the landscape.

Bottle gardeners should check the size of any addition against the circumference of their container opening. No matter how interesting the rock is, it loses its effect caught halfway down the neck of the bottle.

Preparing the Soil Layer

After the plants, soil is the single most important part of a terrarium since it is the medium in which the plants will live and grow. Using the correct potting mix in the beginning may avoid dismantling a planted terrarium after only a short time because soil mix is wrong or drainage inadequate. Sterilized commercial potting mix is available in various sized packages from nurseries, florist shops, variety stores, and even some supermarkets. The other alternative is to make your own soil mix.

Sterilized commercial soils have definite advantages for the novice: you purchase only the amount of soil you need at the time; the soil is already sterilized, contains no pests or weeds, and should be free of any soil disease.

Since most plants adapt readily to a terrarium environment, fertilizers tend to speed up plant growth to an undesirable extent, causing plants to grow lanky or to outgrow the container rapidly. An overgrown terrarium jungle is seldom attractive.

If the plant's original shape (the one the landscape plan used to advantage) is lost, pruning will not always restore it. And since no leaching or evaporation (see page 7) can take place, fertilizers and nutrients are trapped in a terrarium environment. (Leaching is the process in which nutrients and other substances are removed from the topsoil layer by being washed through this layer into subsoil layers; a terrarium contains the equivalent of only a topsoil layer.) Overstimulated plants may even develop fertilizer burn.

Since pruning overgrown plants or removing them is difficult in a bottle and time-consuming in other containers, don't encourage rapid plant growth. Be sure your potting mix isn't too rich and add no fertilizer.

To make your own potting mix, blend equal amounts of coarse river sand, garden loam or good garden topsoil, and leaf mold. To two quarters of this mix, add ½ cup each charcoal and perlite. Spread the mix on baking sheets and sterilize by baking in a 300° oven for at least 30 minutes. A word of warning: baking soil has a very unpleasant odor. Be sure to provide adequate ventilation.

Besides soil, your terrarium will need layers of drainage material and charcoal. A layer of sphagnum moss is optional. The soil will not become watersoaked and the roots will not rot if excess moisture can drain through the soil layer into the drainage layer. Charcoal also provides some drainage and keeps the soil "sweet." (In constantly wet soil, fungi and other organisms cause rot of organic material and generate bad smells and substances that are harmful to plant roots. Wet soil excludes oxygen the roots require.)

Drainage material can consist of crushed rock, pebbles, or broken clay pots. A layer of sphagnum moss, while not necessary, helps keep the soil from sifting into the drainage layer. It will also add some

LAYERS of (A) potting mix, (B) charcoal, and (C) drainage material comprise a viable soil layer.

TERRARIUM TOOLS: (A) metal funnel; (B) watering can; (C) atomizer-type water sprayer; (D) pruning stick with razor blade; (E) stick or dowel; (F) looped wire; (G & H) pick-up tools in 2 lengths; (I) plexiglas tamping tool; (J) bulb baster; (K) bulb-type water sprayer; (L) spoon. See explanation at right.

organic matter to the soil. And charcoal absorbs the noxious by-products of decay.

Charcoal, drainage material, and sphagnum moss can be purchased at nurseries, florist shops, or garden supply stores. Another possible source for these materials is an aquarium supply store.

PLANTING THE TERRARIUM

Once the major planning decisions of finding a location, choosing a container, selecting the plants, and preparing the soil layer are completed, you are ready to plant. Have all the necessary materials assembled and ready to use: cleaned container; soil, charcoal, and drainage material (see page 11-12); tools; and plants.

Allow enough time to complete the project without rushing (estimate the planting time, then "pad it" with an additional hour or so for emergencies). Planting a terrarium, especially one in a bottle, has its pitfalls, and hurrying will only multiply them.

Container Preparation

Sterilize the container at least a day before planting in it. The best method is to run it through a dish-

washer cycle. If this is not possible, wash the container in hot, soapy water and rinse it thoroughly. Detergent film is as unhealthy for plants as it is for people.

Allow the container to dry out completely; soil has a tendency to cling tenaciously to damp glass or plastic. Once a terrarium is planted, this soil may be difficult to remove, especially in a bottle garden. A bottle tends to retain moisture even if dried in a dishwasher; allow it to stand upright for at least 12 hours before planting in it. Stubborn moisture can be removed by directing the air stream from an electric fan or hairdryer directly into the bottle.

If you use a commercial glass cleaner, especially one containing ammonia, allow the container to air for several days to dispel any harmful fumes.

Tools

Many tools are available for planting terrariums. These help you to make holes, add and arrange soil and drainage layers, plant the plants, insert and arrange any decorative objects to be included, and maintain the garden when it is completed. A collection of various tools, some available commercially and some that can be made, is shown at left.

The most versatile tools are long bamboo sticks or pieces of ¼ or ⅜-inch doweling. These can be used to dig holes, move various elements around inside the container, and prop up plants being planted. Add a cork to the end of a stick or dowel and you have a soil tamper; sink a razor blade into the end and you can prune wild leaves or a dead stem. These can be constructed very inexpensively from readily available materials.

Another useful implement can be bought. Called a grabber, pick-up tool, flexible mechanical fingers,

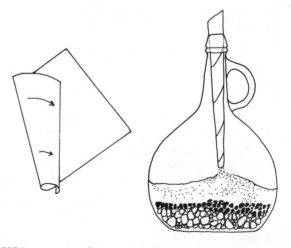

CURL paper or aluminum foil (left) to form a cone; use cone to add parts of soil layer (right).

or astro fingers, it can be purchased in hardware or auto supply stores and is especially useful in planting bottle gardens. Once you have mastered the technique of using it, it can help you to position plants, extract them, or reposition them with ease.

A pair of household scissors can be used for pruning unwieldy plants before they are planted.

An easily-made tool is a wire with a loop fashioned on one end. Similar to the pick-up tool, this wire can also lower plants and remove them, but it requires more dexterity and practice to use. The loop is formed with an opening (see page 16); this enables you to set a plant in its prepared hole, tamp it down, and remove the wire by working the opening around the stem.

Another tool that can be made is the plexiglas rod. A flat piece of plexiglas is cut approximately ½-inch wide, then one end is bent into an L-shape. This tool is used for tamping soil around the plant roots and for arranging various terrarium elements. Making this tool requires equipment especially designed for working with plexiglas.

Soil and drainage layer elements can be put into the container by various methods. A large kitchen spoon works well in open containers. For bottles or jugs, a kitchen funnel or a cone fashioned out of paper or aluminum foil will do the job. Any of the longer tools, the pick-up tool, a stick or dowel, the plexiglas rod, or the looped wire will be useful in arranging the drainage, charcoal, and potting mix and creating a slope or terracing the landscape.

Watering the planted terrarium is best accomplished by special tools. An atomizer or bulb-shaped sprayer will create a fine mist and won't overpower tender plants or ones that are delicately anchored. A kitchen bulb baster enables the water to be directed to specific areas or hard-to-reach corners.

Watering a bottle is best accomplished with a narrow-necked watering can (see page 15). This method of watering allows you to measure the water precisely and also helps clean the glass or plastic sides of the container after planting.

Maintaining a terrarium makes use of some of the same tools. Dead plants in a bottle can be removed

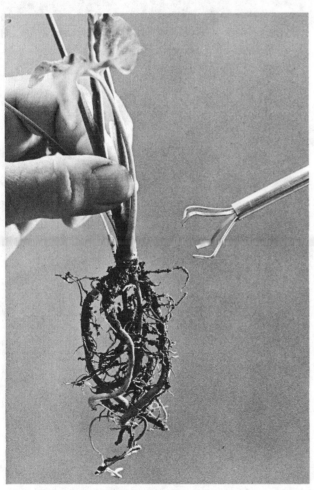

GRASP and secure plant at stem end or crown with pick-up tool. Avoid closing tool claw completely.

INSERT plant roots first with pick-up tool. Lower plant to prepared hole and release it.

HOW TO PLANT A BOTTLE GARDEN

1. ASSEMBLE EVERYTHING, have ready for planting: cleaned container; plants; tools; soil components.

2. FUNNEL or paper cone (see page 12) directs charcoal into bottle, keeps dust away from bottle sides.

3. STICK or dowel is useful for arranging soil layer. Use to form slopes or for other landscaping details.

4. STRIKE nursery pot against working surface to dislodge plant. Support plant and remove carefully.

5. DIRECT PLANT ROOTS *first into bottle with a pick-up tool. Guide leaves through opening carefully.*

6. TAMP *plants into place firmly, gently. Place tallest plants first, then smaller ones, ground covers.*

7. CAREFULLY *hit leaves with stick to shake off the dirt particles. Spread ground covers to fill in area.*

8. WATER *bottle sparingly. With your fingers, direct water flow down container sides to wash them.*

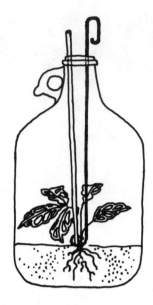

SLIP opening of looped wire tool around plant stem (left). Insert plant roots-first and lower it to prepared hole (right). Hold plant with stick and remove looped wire.

with the pick-up tool or the looped wire. Gently displace the plant (try not to disturb surrounding plants) from the soil and remove it root-end first. Prune overgrown leaves or dead or damaged stems with the razor stick by sawing them off or carefully pinch them off with the pick-up tool. Remove all refuse with the pick-up tool.

Adding the Soil Layer

The first items put into the container are 1) drainage material, 2) charcoal, and 3) the planting mix. Approximately ¼ of the container space will be devoted to this layer (see Preparing the Soil, page 11, for additional information).

Allotting ¼ of the space in the container for the soil layer is a good rule-of-thumb to apply. For example, a 12-inch bottle should have a 3-inch soil layer. Divide the soil layer into ⅜-inch drainage material; a thin layer of charcoal (enough to cover the drainage material); a thin layer of sphagnum moss, if used; approximately 2⅛-inches planting mix. This is the minimum soil layer. If a slope or additional landscaping is planned, add more planting mix to fill in the design.

First, put in the layer of drainage material. Small gravel or crushed rock, perlite, sponge rock (lava rock), or even broken bits of clay pots will serve equally well. If you are planting a bottle garden, make sure the drainage material is in small enough pieces to go through the opening. Use a kitchen funnel or a piece of paper or aluminum foil fashioned into a cone shape (see page 12). The funnel or cone channels the drainage material (and the other soil

layer additions) into the container, keeping it away from container sides. This will reduce later cleanup.

Next add a thin layer of charcoal. Put in enough to completely cover the drainage layer. Pour charcoal slowly; the fine, black dust that is created can be hard to remove from container sides.

If you plan to use the sphagnum moss layer, prepare it first. Moss is usually purchased in dried form. Soak it in water overnight, then squeeze out as much moisture as possible. To insert it into a bottle, cut the moss into small pieces. Overlap the small pieces to create a solid layer. Leaving the pieces as large as the opening of the container makes the moss layer more cohesive and effectively separates the soil from the drainage-charcoal layer.

Next, add the planting mix, pouring it slowly through a funnel or paper cone. You will find the mix easier to work with if it is slightly damp. Bone-dry mix is hard to moisten later. It tends to float when watered heavily, and bottle gardens look strange with a water line. When planting a bottle, the mix should be dry enough to pour easily through the funnel or cone but still not be bone-dry. Add enough water to the mix to attain the desired moisture level before placing it in the container.

Once the minimum soil layer has been added (¼ of the container space filled), consider the landscaping. Plants on different levels—on a slope, a terrace, or a central knoll—appear much more intriguing than those planted on a flat garden plot (see page 20). More planting mix should be added to the minimum soil layer to achieve various levels of planting surfaces. Slopes backed up to container sides are the easiest in small containers; terracing (several levels

UNDERWATER GARDENS

An underwater garden in an aquarium is an intriguing place, with or without fish. Used in conjunction with other gardens or groups of potted plants, it can provide needed humidity. If you have fish, the plants will make the habitat seem more natural, provide hiding places for the fish and eggs, and reduce the chance of excessive algae growth. Plants were once included for their oxygen-giving function, but aerators have now eliminated this need.

Before planting your aquatic garden, wash the gravel or very coarse sand thoroughly, then spread several inches of it on the container bottom. Petrified wood, aquarium rocks, or driftwood can decorate the landscape. Then, holding the sand or gravel in place with heavy paper, slowly pour in water until the tank is one-third full. Set rooted and bunched aquarium plants in the sand and fill tank to about elbow depth until the landscape is arranged to your satisfaction. Floating plants can be added to the tank at any time.

If the aquarium is for plants only, it won't need a cover, and the water temperature can be kept around 65°. Fish will require temperatures of around 75°. Special light units for many tank sizes can be purchased at aquarium stores, but a grouping of plants alone will thrive in natural light. Too much sun, though, can cause algae to form on the glass.

Cleaning algae off glass sides, occasional pruning of aquarium plants, and replacing evaporated water is all the care that an aquatic garden requires. Fish, of course, will need regular feedings.

Plants that grow under water are not in their normal environment but will thrive if given proper conditions. The plants listed below are some of the least demanding, but, depending on the conditions you provide for them, some of these will do better than others. Most can be propagated by stem cuttings, so start with a sampling of several that you like and propagate the plants that grow most successfully.

Amblystegium riparium. Tiny, pale green leaves on threadlike stems distinguish this moss that can be anchored to the bottom, wood, or rocks, or can float on the water surface.

Anacharis canadensis (Elodea). Rapid growing, soft-stemmed plants will become leggy with insufficient light. Fish will eat it, but it grows back rapidly.

Azolla caroliniana. This small, floating plant has tiny leaves and multiplies rapidly.

Cabomba caroliniana (fanwort). Long roots form on this plant with finely divided leaves. It makes a good hiding place for fish, needs plenty of strong light, and prefers cold water.

Ceratopteris thalictroides (water sprite). As this plant grows to the surface, new plants develop from buds which arise from all parts of the leaves and the portion planted in the bottom dies off. Grows rapidly in good light.

Cryptocoryne. Large varied genus of beautiful plants. Do not like frequent replanting.

C. cordata. Warm water plant where light is limited. Lance-shaped leaves are olive green above, reddish purple beneath. Plants send out runner with new plantlets at end.

Echinodorus (Amazon sword plants). Many oblong or lance-shaped leaves rise from a central crown. Delicate leaves are vulnerable to damage by plant-eating snails. If algae grows on the leaf surface, plants are getting too much light. If inner leaves turn brown, more light is needed. Large species are grown singly in large tanks, but the Dwarf Amazon and other small species form thick stands with many runners.

Eichhornia (water hyacinth). Upright blue spikes form on this flowering plant. Its unusual leaves and long roots are a favorite shelter for fish.

Hygrophila polysperma. Produces pairs of oblong leaves from central stem and will grow to the surface of most home tanks. Widely used, fast-growing, hardy plant. Pale green foliage contrasts with the dark green of other plants.

Microsorium (Java fern). Hardy plant that is attractive growing from pieces of tree root, as well as anchored to the bottom.

Nymphoides aquatica (underwater banana). Plant is usually floated to show roots that resemble a bunch of bananas. Pale green or reddish brown roundish leaves.

Nymphaea (water lilies). Beautiful plants need space to open out. *N. sagittifolium* and *N. japonicum* are longest lasting and most decorative. *N. pumilum* is a dwarf.

Riccia fluitans (crystalwort). Bright green cushions float just beneath the water surface. Some tropical fish lay eggs in it; young like to hide in it.

Sagittaria (arrowhead). Hardy grasslike foliage requires plenty of light. Occasional small flowers.

Synnema triflorum (water wisteria). This plant grows fast under strong light. Large, deeply lobed leaves form rosettes. Suckers can be cut and rooted elsewhere. A good floating plant.

Vallisneria spiralis (eel or tape grass). Narrow or undulating or spiral leaves rise from a central crown. Good light but not too strong. Spreads by runners. Hardy but do not plant too deep.

REMOVE plant from nursery pot and shake off excess soil. Loosely pack remaining soil around roots.

PLACE root ball on paper or cloth toweling and gently roll it up to form a solid core.

of planting surfaces) requires a large container. A tank-type terrarium (usually a converted aquarium) allows enough space for the amateur landscape architect to experiment.

Planting the Terrarium

Creating a miniature landscape in a small container can be time consuming, tricky—even exasperating. The space is limited and difficult to work in, and learning to manipulate the tools takes practice. But, like learning to eat with chopsticks, the art of handling terrarium tools can be mastered. And once the terrarium is planted, all your effort is rewarded: a garden under glass will provide endless pleasure throughout its lifetime.

The order in which you plant depends upon the landscaping plan chosen. The easiest method is to secure the focal plant first (usually the tallest plant), then arrange the other plants around it. Normally medium-height plants are positioned after tall ones, then the ground covers are placed.

If a rock, a piece of driftwood, or some other object is to be an integral part of the landscape, position it first. Bottle gardeners should be sure the object is small enough to pass through the bottle opening before planning their garden around it.

REMOVE PLANT from toweling when core is solid. Compact core will be easy to insert into container.

TINTED glass bottle needs plants with bold leaf patterns. Plants (see diagram, right): (A) Pteris; (B) Syngonium podophyllum; (C) Hedera helix; (D) Saxifraga sarmentosa; (E) Selaginella.

PLANTS THRIVE in the ideal condition this water bottle offers. Plants (see diagram, right): (A) Pilea cadierei; (B) Dracaena sanderiana; (C) Codiaeum aucubaefolium; (D) Selaginella.

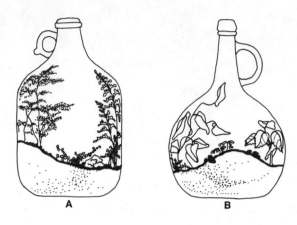

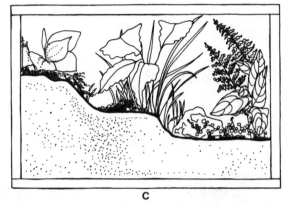

FORM LANDSCAPES with additional potting mix. Slopes (A), knolls (B), terraces (C) are most common.

Plant the focal plant. Prepare a hole in the soil with a stick or tamper tool. Remove the plant from its nursery pot by striking the pot sharply against a hard surface, dislodging the plant. Brace the plant with your fingers (see photo on page 14, lower right-hand corner), turn it upside down, and pull it free of the pot. Remove excess soil, leaving the soil around the root ball intact. Form a soil core by rolling the root ball in paper or cloth toweling (see photos on page 18). Insert the plant, roots first, with the pick-up tool or the looped wire, placing it in the prepared hole and gently tamping the soil around the roots (see pages 13 and 16).

If you are planting a bottle or a container with a difficult opening, be sure the leaves of each plant are flexible enough to permit it to pass through the opening. Once the plant is in the bottle, use a stick or pick-up tool to maneuver the root end of the plant into the hole (since you're working at a distance this can be difficult) and gently tamp the soil around the roots. Be sure the first plant is secured before planting other plants. A picture sequence of planting a bottle garden is on pages 14-15.

Plant remaining plants in the same manner described above. One thing to remember: don't crowd the plants closely together; give them room to grow.

Sometimes bottle gardeners may uproot one plant while attempting to secure another. If this happens, don't lose patience. Carefully replace the uprooted plant, tamp it down, and continue working.

If, during the planting, you find a different plant placement is better than the original plan, feel free to change it. Don't be bound by your prearranged landscape; use it merely as a guideline.

Establishing the Rain Cycle

Adding the moisture which starts the rain cycle is the final task of terrarium planting. This initial watering is crucial, especially in a bottle garden. Since terrarium drainage is limited and little moisture is lost through evaporation (see page 7), excess moisture is difficult to remove. If given too much water, plant roots cannot get oxygen and literally drown. Like a good martini, a terrarium is best on the dry side. More water can always be added later if needed. Overwatering is the major cause of terrarium failure.

Watering serves a dual purpose. It adds sufficient moisture for normal plant growth and establishes the atmosphere of humidity and the rain cycle (see page 7) that makes closed terrariums unique. It is also useful in cleaning inaccessible container sides after the planting. If the planting mix was moist to begin with, add a maximum of 2 oz. (¼ cup) water for containers of 1 gallon or less and 4 oz. (½ cup) water for larger containers. If the mix was on the dry side, moisten it thoroughly.

Moisture levels can be easily tested in accessible containers. Test the soil with your finger—if it is dry about 1 inch below the soil surface, add water. Closed, inaccessible containers need careful watching. If the plants begin to droop or the soil appears parched, rewater sparingly.

The water used can be regular tap water at room temperature. Measure the amount needed into a watering can or another container, and let it stand for several hours to bring the water to room temperature. If your tap water is high in minerals or other chemicals, use bottled spring or distilled water. Again, let it sit for several hours before using. Never use softened water. If you have a water softener, always draw water for your plants from an outside faucet or use bottled water.

A fine mist sprayer is one of the best watering tools for containers. It waters the entire planting area without overwatering any one spot. A bulb baster allows watering the roots of individual plants, but the small amount of water required for a terrarium may be difficult to divide among the plants equally.

When watering a bottle garden, take special care. Little moisture will evaporate through the small opening. A watering can with a narrow spout works well. Measure the water into the can, then direct the flow of water against the neck of the bottle with your

VIVARIUM GARDENS

If your child can't resist bringing home captured frogs, snakes, or lizards, or if he would like a turtle from a pet store, combine his interest in natural history with a terrarium garden.

The best container for your vivarium is a tank aquarium. Tanks ranging from 5 to 15-gallons in size are best, but any large glass or plastic container can be used.

Plant the vivarium like any terrarium garden. Place gravel on the bottom of a cleaned container and cover it with sterilized, commercial potting mix. Deep sand should be provided for animals that like to burrow.

Sink a dish for water. Since it will have to be removed for cleaning, plants should not be set so close to the dish that they would interfere.

Except for feeding, animals will take care of themselves in this environment, providing it is not overcrowded. If an animal looks unhealthy, it is best to set it free. For information on the various animals and their needs, contact your local pet store. Because the container will not be entirely covered, plants will need occasional water.

A desert setting (best for lizards, horned toads, snakes) is probably the easiest to establish and maintain. Cover the bottom with sand, add rocks for sunning, a succulent or cactus, and a water dish. Keep the vivarium in a warm, sunny location.

If not enough sun is available to maintain a temperature over 65°, provide the warmth of a 60 watt incandescent light bulb for 10 hours a day. Rocks and caves for hiding and sand for burrowing are required to give the inmates an occasional escape from this light.

The woodland setting (good for chameleons, frogs, salamanders, snakes, toads) provides a moist but not saturated climate. This environment needs filtered sun or an overhead light, moderate temperatures, and about 50% humidity. Moisture-loving terrarium plants such as fittonia and most tropicals will thrive here.

The aqua-terrarium (for turtles, tadpoles, newts, frogs) combines water and land for amphibians and other water lovers. They need swimming room as well as a place to sun. So that both plants and animals will be happy, the water and land must be separated. A rubber seal around a glass partition from the container bottom to the water level will serve this purpose. An alternative to the partition is to plant aquarium plants (see page 17) in sand and place large, protruding rocks for sunning and climbing.

This type of vivarium requires the most maintenance, since the water must be kept clean. An aquarium filter under the gravel will help, but you'll still have to change the water occasionally.

AQUA-TERRARIUM GARDEN recreates a natural setting for the turtles and enhances the watching for the small observer. Plants are Pilea depressa, Chamaedorea elegans.

TERRARIUM ON ITS SIDE resembles a ship-in-a-bottle. Planting a garden in a clear wine bottle is for advanced bottle gardeners; deft fingers are needed. Plants are Pilea depressa.

fingers (see page 15). Water will run down the sides of the container to help wash away any dirt or dust still clinging to the sides down into the soil layer. This method also disperses the water evenly. The various watering implements are pictured on page 12.

If after careful attention you still overwater a bit, the signal will be extreme fogging of the glass or plastic sides. The only remedy is to remove the excess moisture rapidly by uncovering the terrarium until the garden dries to a normal level. Then recover it and enjoy your handiwork.

Ridding a saturated bottle garden of excess water is more difficult. One method is to wrap paper towels around a rod or stick and place it into the bottle so that it touches the soil. This soaks up excess water by capillary action. Keep blotting with additional towels until extra moisture is gone. Another method is to direct the cool air flow of an electric fan or hair dryer into the bottle. This will speed up the exchange of dry air for the moist air contained in the bottle.

MAINTAINING THE TERRARIUM

Terrarium demands are nothing compared to the constant garden chores of lawn mowing, leaf raking, and weeding. Complaining of sore muscles or an aching back from terrarium maintenance will gain you little sympathy. Upon completion, a terrarium itself takes on the major responsibility of controlling its interior temperature and keeping the moisture level constant. The rest is up to you.

Periodic checks for proper light and correct moisture level are necessary for a healthy garden, as are inspections to find overgrown or ailing plants to be pruned or replaced and pests or plant diseases to be dealt with. The tiny garden of Eden that is so charming viewed through the glass can quickly develop into a paradise lost if left untended.

Proper Lighting

Correct lighting (see page 8) is essential to maintaining a healthy garden. The natural light source constantly changes with the seasons. If the amount of light your terrarium receives is drastically diminished, move it to a lighter spot or provide some artificial lighting (see page 39).

Another light-related problem is *tropism*, an unbalanced plant growth. If the plants in your terrarium begin to resemble the leaning tower of Pisa, tropism is the culprit; it causes plants to lean toward the window or light source. This uneven growth is created by swelling plant cells on the dark side of the plant. This is a sort of plant protest, requesting its fair share of available light.

Tropism can be corrected by occasionally turning the container so that all sides have an equal opportunity at the light, a major undertaking if you've planted a 50-gallon tank. Another corrective measure is to provide artificial overhead lighting (see page 39). Once the light is distributed evenly, plants should maintain symmetrical, upright growth.

Watering

A closed terrarium shouldn't require additional watering for several months. Periodically, about

ELONGATED WATER BOTTLE provides a wide planting area with good visibility. Plants are: (A) Chamaedorea elegans; (B) Hedera helix; (C) Asparagus setaceus; (D) Peperomia caperata.

ACCESSORIES FOR THIS GARDEN planted in a misshapen water bottle are artificial florist's moss and assorted rocks. Plants are: (A) Fatsia japonica; (B) Aglaonema modestum; (C) Selaginella.

If you don't have a greenhouse, the constant humidity and protection provided by a covered glass garden can serve to propagate plants by seeds or cuttings as well as to take care of plants while you're away; you can even harvest a crop of alfalfa sprouts.

An endless variety of containers for these tiny greenhouses can be improvised—from flats or aquarium tanks covered with glass or plastic to pots or soil contained in a plastic bag. A glass jar or glass inverted over a plant or cutting is another method.

Seed Propagation. The most common reason for failure of seeds to germinate is lack of sufficient moisture, especially for very fine seeds. A glass or plastic cover that lets light through and retains moisture is an ideal solution to this problem. Moisten the planting medium well and tamp it down before sowing the seeds. For very fine seeds, use chopped sphagnum moss, scattering seeds on the top. Place the covered container in good light but not in direct sun. No additional water should be needed until the seeds have sprouted.

When the seeds have sprouted, remove the cover and water with a mist spray when needed. Replace the cover at night for warmth.

Cactus seeds are particularly susceptible to fungus attacks; use sterilized sphagnum moss or brick dust that cannot host a fungus for the sprouting medium. Sprinkle the seeds on top of the medium and cover container with a pane of glass or sheet of plastic. It may take as long as a year before the seedlings are ready for transplanting; fertilize lightly at about four months.

Propagation by Cuttings. Many plants can be easily propagated from cuttings, and these too need continual moisture to root successfully.

Remove leaves that go below the rooting medium and cut off part of those that are particularly large. Too many leaves require more water than the cuttings can take up, causing it to wilt. Applying a rooting hormone to the base of the cutting will increase your chances of success. If condensation on the glass or plastic cover is too heavy, provide ventilation. Pot your cuttings when they show new growth, continuing to give them cool tempera-

SEEDS GERMINATE when sealed in plastic bag. Bag, like a terrarium, holds in moisture, humidity.

TO PROPAGATE CUTTINGS, put soil in plastic, add moisture, seal. Pot when new growth appears.

tures, shade, and humidity until they are well established.

House Plants. If you worry about your house plants while you're away for any length of time, an improvised plastic cover will keep them moist up to a month.

First, soak the soil well, then allow the excess moisture to drain away. Put the entire pot in a plastic bag and twist or tie the top to seal it. A garment bag from the cleaners, held away from the foliage by stakes in the soil, is useful for larger plants or a grouping of pots. If the plant is too big for this, wrap plastic around the pot, sealing the top around the plant stems to prevent moisture loss from the soil.

The plastic will create a terrarium atmosphere, providing the plant with humidity and moisture until you return.

Covered Food Gardens. Growing food in a glass garden can allow you to harvest fresh crops throughout the year. Alfalfa, wheat, and other seeds are easy to sprout in a glass jar and have many uses in cooking. These seeds are usually avail-

able at health food or natural food stores.

Soak the seeds overnight in a 1 to 2-quart jar in just enough water to cover the seeds. Drain off the water in the morning (covering the opening with cheesecloth and holding the cloth in place with a jar ring or rubber band). Rinse seeds twice a day with cool water through the cloth strainer top. Drain thoroughly each time and return jar to its side.

When the leaves appear, give the sprouts more light to make them green but never place them in direct sunlight. When most of the sprouts have leaves, seal the jar and refrigerate. They will keep in the refrigerator up to a week.

Hospital for Ailing Plants. If a favorite plant suddenly begins to droop or die, cover it with an inverted glass jar, a bell dome (see page 26), or tie a plastic bag around it. The improvised cover will provide the plant with humidity and constant moisture. Unless your problem stems from pests, plant disease, or intolerable growing conditions, the temporary removal to an ideal climate should put your plant back on its roots.

SPROUTED ALFALFA seeds are good in salads, sandwiches. Sealed in glass jar, seeds sprout easily.

INVERT A JAR or water glass over a sick plant. Constant humidity and moisture may revive it.

BELL DOME (background) and fruit jar with lid provide terrarium atmospheres. Both conserve humidity, moisture.

GLASS EGG becomes a novel terrarium. Removable top makes it accessible. Plant is Podocarpus macrophyllus.

every two months, check accessible gardens by feeling the soil; add water if the soil feels dry ½ to 1 inch below the surface. If excessive condensation fogs the garden after watering, treat the container for extra moisture as described on page 22.

You'll find no foolproof method for checking the moisture level in a bottle garden. Some intuitive green thumbers claim they can tell when a terrarium needs water by the weight of the bottle (if the bottle feels lighter than normal, they add water); others tap the containers and the pitch of the resounding "thunk" tells them if more water is needed. These are methods used by expert plantsmen.

A more reliable method for the novice is a visual one. Observe your garden closely. If condensation shows on the container sides, the moisture cycle is at work. A lack of condensation signals you to watch the garden carefully for further signs of thirst. Look at the plants themselves; if they droop or appear brittle, they probably need water. Another indication that moisture has evaporated is parched-looking soil. If the signs point to a thirsty terrarium, add water sparingly (see page 20 for guidelines).

Watch for excessive condensation in the container. If the view of the garden becomes completely obscured, condensation is excessive. Treat as directed on page 22. (Remember, overwatering is the major cause of terrarium failure.)

A word of warning: watering does not cure all terrarium ills. If one or two plants seem to be drooping but the rest of the garden appears healthy enough, check other possibilities before adding water. Yellow leaves, burned leaf edges, plant droop, and other symptoms can be caused by various problems: too much light, not enough light, a pest attack, plant diseases, too much moisture, not enough moisture. Investigate the problem thoroughly before draining the watering can into the container.

Pruning and Plant Replacement

Vigorous growth is not a desirable trait for terrarium plants. Since the plants are small to begin with, a certain amount of growth is necessary to fill in the landscape and to allow the garden to take on an established appearance. But often, in the limited confines of a terrarium, plants outgrow the design or become misshapen. Pruning trims them down to size and removes unsightly yellow leaves, spent blossoms, and dead branches. It also keeps plants shaped and sized in proportion to the desired landscape.

Pruning is an easy matter in an accessible container. It can be accomplished with your hands or with a small pair of scissors. Snip off the offending leaf or branch and discard it.

Bottle gardens present a greater pruning problem. The inaccessibility of plants necessitates special tools and careful handling. The best implements for pruning in a bottle are the pick-up tool and a stick with a razor blade or some other cutting edge attached (see page 12). The pick-up tool actually squeezes undesirable appendages off; the blade or cutting edge severs branches and leaves. Use the pick-up tool to remove pruning debris.

Sometimes a plant can't be pruned to shape or becomes so large it dwarfs the rest of the garden. Removing the plant altogether is the best solution. In an accessible garden, pull the plant out by hand or remove it with a spoon and replace it with a new, healthy plant. In bottle gardens, remove it with the pick-up tool or the looped wire (see page 12). Snare the unwieldy plant near the steam base and extract it roots first. (Removal by the roots first helps keep the root ball and leaves from breaking apart and littering the garden when the plant is pulled through the opening.) Once the plant is out, it can be repotted for use in the house or discarded.

Pests and Plant Diseases

A terrarium garden's isolation protects it from outside insect attacks. In a garden, most pest problems are planted along with the plants. Pests may hide in root balls, or insect eggs may be present in mosses or on other plants. Identification and extermination information for common pests is given on page 37.

Mold (a type of gray fungus) is the most common terrarium plant disease. Its most frequent cause is overwatering. Mold can also be introduced by planting an infected plant or a plant not suited to terrarium environment. The moist, humid atmosphere created in a terrarium is the perfect environment for molds to develop, and the garden will quickly succumb to it if not treated in time.

The best cure for mold is removal of the diseased plant. If the mold is more widespread, remove and replace all the diseased plants or dismantle the entire terrarium and replant it. Discard all infected plants.

If mold plagues your gardens continually, spray plants *before planting them* with a spray of dust-type fungicide. (Read package directions carefully. Certain plants are susceptible to damage by spray ingredients.) Do not direct the spray into a bottle garden. This covers the container sides with a spray film that is difficult to remove.

Any container in which the sides can be protected with paper or some other type of shield can be sprayed directly. Leave the lid off the garden for a short time to allow fumes to escape.

13-GALLON WATER BOTTLE *is perfect for large ferns. Normal-sized bottle in foreground compares size.*

TWO AQUARIUM TANKS *placed top to top form a terrarium for large plants. This one encases an orchid.*

BRANDY SNIFTERS and open globes (above)
are perfect containers for miniature gardens.
Clear glass allows easy visibility. Rough ceramic
container (right), rocks, and driftwood serve as a
background for cactus and succulent planting.

Miniature Gardens

The mobility and versatility of miniature gardens are two qualities that attract the indoor green-thumber. A large variety of available containers and a broad selection of suitable plants allow any style and kind of garden to be created.

Being small and independently contained, a miniature garden can be moved to decorate or accent any part of your house. From serving as the centerpiece at a dinner party to decorating a coffee table, mantel, window sill, bookcase, shelf, or even cheering a sick room, the uses of the diminutive garden are many. The only condition a location must meet is to provide enough light for normal plant growth.

The versatility of a miniature garden stems in large part from the many possible containers that can be used. Glass or plastic cubes, brandy snifters, open globes; ceramic pots and flat dishes; subtle bonsai pots; elegant brass or metal containers; even clay pots make up the vast selection. The image you wish the garden to portray will depend on the type of container you select.

While the container adds to the garden's appearance, the appropriateness of the landscape to both the container and the location is vital in creating the total effect of the garden. Choose plants that are compatible in similar garden situations, that are complimentary in color, form, and interest, and that combine nicely in a landscape design. Each element of the total garden is equally important.

With a suitable container, good location, correct plant selection, and well planned landscape, a miniature garden offers the indoor gardener an opportunity to create an object of horticultural beauty.

This book defines a miniature garden as a group of plants artfully arranged in a partly open or open container. Unlike the terrarium garden discussed in Chapter 1, "Terrariums," the miniature garden has no controlled climate; the gardener has to provide the water, humidity, and any other vital necessities.

Because almost any climate can be provided, the gardener is free to choose from a wide variety of plants. As long as the garden contains plants with similar needs, it can include tropical humidity lovers; cool, shade, and moisture-loving forest inhabitants; or desert cactus and succulents.

Before the actual planting can take place, though, your garden will need some planning. When all the design details have been mapped out and the necessary purchases have been made, you can begin your project of creating a miniature garden.

PLANNING THE MINIATURE GARDEN

What is involved in planning for your miniature garden? Finding a location that will meet all the garden's needs, as well as displaying the landscape to its best advantage; choosing a container to house the garden and compliment the landscape design, as well as the container's location; selecting plants that contrast in color, form, and growth habit, yet blend together nicely in the landscape design and are compatible enough to thrive in the same garden environment; and providing the correct soil layer in which the plants can flourish: all these parts, carefully planned and put together, should create a miniature garden that will give lasting pleasure.

CLAY POTS shaped like animals make casual containers for miniature gardens. Most are of red clay.

PIG-SHAPED POT is a clever herb garden for a rustic kitchen. Fresh parsley is pretty and practical.

Finding a Location

Because of the versatility and mobility of a miniature garden, it need not be limited to a certain location. The same garden that graces your coffee table can easily enhance the mantel or serve as the centerpiece for a dinner party. But if the garden is to remain in one spot for any length of time, the location will need to provide sufficient light to sustain normal plant growth and a fairly constant temperature.

The amount of light needed will vary with the plants themselves. Each garden grouping should contain plants with similar light requirements (see Selecting the Plants, page 33). The light requirement of various plants are listed in the Plant Selection Guide, pages 44-79. If you are unsure of the proper light requirement, choose a location with bright light but no direct sun. A north window is ideal.

If the plants need additional light, consider "sunning" them in a brighter spot for a few hours each day or providing them with artificial light (see page 39).

Most plants are able to adapt to normal house temperatures that are kept fairly constant (a slight drop of a few degrees at night time is not harmful). Certain conditions should be avoided, though. Plants, like people, should never sit in drafts. And never set a garden too near a heat register: too much heat can be as harmful as too little. If there is danger of frost, a miniature garden near a window should be protected; a drawn curtain or newspapers can serve as a shield.

The location chosen can affect your landscape design. A garden to be viewed from all sides needs a different composition from a garden to be positioned where only one side will be visible. One placed on a low table should be as interesting viewed from the top as from the sides. A planting perched high on a bookcase or shelf can be twice as intriguing with a plant dangling over the edge. A good landscape design should enhance the proposed location as well as create a pleasing garden.

Choosing a Container

Finding the right container to house your miniature garden can be as enjoyable and challenging as the actual garden planting. Many containers that meet planting requirements are readily available, and the selection of dishes and pots in various sizes, styles, and colors is extensive. Most containers are glass or ceramic; interesting plastic and metal ones can also be considered.

A miniature garden container should be at least 3 inches deep. The dish needs to hold layers of potting mix, charcoal, and drainage material and

CONTAINER *for small landscape has one side with drainage for planting, one side to hold water.*

provide a substantial base for a plant's root system. Too little soil can cause stunted plant growth, or the plant may topple over, lacking a firm foundation. If a container has less than 3 inches of depth, a drainage hole is a necessity.

Providing adequate drainage for the garden is your second consideration in choosing a container. This can be accomplished in two ways: the bottom of the container can be perforated to allow excess water to drain away; or a layer of drainage material positioned underneath the soil layer can retain it.

While a drainage hole in the container bottom efficiently rids the garden of its excess moisture, a saucer or tray must be provided to catch the runoff. Although some containers can be purchased with matching saucers, for most containers the gardener must find a suitable receptacle. Without a saucer or some other device to hold the excess water, you run the risk of ruining your furniture. Look for unobtrusive saucers or trays. A mismatched saucer may protect furniture surfaces but ruin the visual effect of the garden. Pads or mats can be used for protection but are also visually jarring.

An alternate method of draining the garden is to provide a layer of drainage material inside the container. Placed beneath layers of potting mix and charcoal, the drainage material (see page 33) allows water to seep through the soil layers into the drainage layer. This keeps plant roots from sitting in soggy soil. Even if the container has a drainage layer, water the garden cautiously. Overwatering causes more miniature garden failures than any other factor.

Look for containers at nurseries, florist shops, garden supply centers, import stores, or nurseries

VARIOUS BONSAI POTS *all make interesting containers. Deep pots can accommodate a wide range of plants. Cactus and succulents do well in shallower pots, as do bonsai trees, bonsai groves, or a rock landscape.*

GARDEN WITH A MOAT

If your interests include both gardening and aquariums, why not combine them and make this unique container? Here you'll have the best of both plant and fish worlds. The see-through sides reflect the various images with a kaleidoscope effect. And the plants should thrive because the surrounding water will provide humidity.

For materials, go to a plastic supply store. You'll need a 2 by 3-foot sheet of ⅜-inch thick acrylic plastic, acrylic cement (ethylene dichloride), and an applicator (brush, eyedropper, or hypodermic applicator). Cut the plastic into one 12 by 12-inch piece for the base, four 5 by 8½-inch pieces for the planter, and four 7 by 12-inch pieces for the tank. Have these cut at the store or do it yourself, using a blade with teeth that are close set like those of a hack saw. Support the plastic firmly as you cut, leaving the masking paper on until you're ready to glue.

Other materials can come from the hardware store or your workbench: two 3-inch C-clamps and two corner clamps; weights such as bricks or books; sandpaper (several grades down to 600 grit); a square; a ¼-inch drill; scrap wood; vise.

Sand the edges of the cut plastic, using progressively finer grades of sandpaper. Check frequently with a square; edges must be straight and square to be leakproof. Drill a ¼-inch drain hole for the planter in the center of the base piece with a hand or power drill.

Before gluing, practice making joints on scrap plastic. Then hold two sides together with two corner clamps and apply glue to the joint. Use enough cement to drive out any air and wipe up any spills. Wait 2 hours before removing clamps.

Cement the two glued sides of the planter box to the base by setting them in position and applying cement under the bottom edges. Weight the upper edges to hold them in place until the glue dries. Assemble the other side of the planter and the sides of the fish tank in the same way, gluing two sides together at a time.

Let joints dry about 6 hours before testing for leaks by filling tank with water. If no leaks appear, empty the tank and plant; clean up any spilled soil, then fill fish tank. When choosing fish, remember that goldfish need least care; more exotic fish require an aerator, filter, and heater.

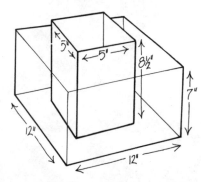

DRAWING shows size of the various plastic pieces.

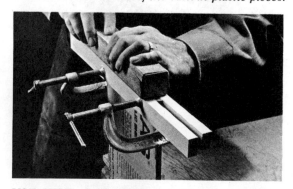

USE VISE, C-CLAMPS to hold plastic sides in place. Block sander will smooth rough edges.

AQUARIUM-PLANTER has see-through sides. Fish swim around planter which holds Adiantum.

specializing in bonsai or indoor gardening.

If you want a really unique container, make your own. Ideas and directions for clay containers are given on pages 34-35. A plexiglas garden/aquarium combination is described on page 32.

Selecting the Plants

The best insurance for planting a miniature garden that will last is choosing plants that are healthy and compatible with each other. Selecting a variety of plant types, such as tall plants, medium-sized ones, and ground covers that will complement one another in an arrangement is also a consideration. If careful attention is given to this initial plant selection, your landscaped garden has a good chance of pleasing you for a long time to come.

The Plant Selection Guide, pages 44-79, is a good source of plant information. Plants are described, and their various requirements for type of light and soil and preferred amounts of humidity and water are given. Studying this guide will allow you to make good plant selections when you are confronted with tables crowded with tiny plants in a nursery or garden center.

In looking for healthy plants, check their leaves and root systems for signs of improper care or growth. Here are some warning signs: roots growing out of the drainage hole or ones that are visible on the soil surface (this shows that the plant is pot bound); leaves and stems that show signs of pests or pest attacks; plants with pale or yellow lower leaves or leaves with brown edges; leggy or sparse growth. If the plant selected shows none of the above symptoms, it should be a healthy specimen, and healthy plants constitute a healthy garden.

Plant compatibility means choosing plants that will thrive together in similar soil, light, humidity, and watering conditions. Plants should respond well in a group planting. Since the gardens are small, special treatment for a particular plant is difficult to provide. Individual plant requirements are listed in the Plant Selection Guide, pages 44-79.

Always take your container with you when you shop for plants (see Choosing a Container, page 30). You can easily judge the number and size of plants your container can hold.

To create a pleasing garden arrangement, plants not only need to be healthy and compatible, they also need to complement each other in the landscape. Use basic landscaping rules to arrange the garden. Choose plants that vary in height, leaf structure, and color or variegation of foliage.

Decide on the plant arrangement before you begin the actual planting. The best time for this is while the plants are still in their nursery pots (see page 10). Select one plant, perhaps the tallest one or one with bold leaves or a striking pattern, then

SOIL LAYER for garden without drain hole: (A) potting mix, (B) charcoal, and (C) drainage material.

arrange the other plants around it. Work with the plants until you create a finished landscape that is pleasing to your eye.

Now is the time to decide on garden accents. If an interesting rock or an unusual piece of driftwood is to be the garden's focal point, arrange your landscape around it. If tiny pebbles or rocks are to serve as finishing touches, be sure to leave a border of unplanted ground to incorporate them nicely. Anything used as an accent, besides the plants, should promote the naturalness of the setting. Don't overdo the ornamentation; let nature's simplicity be your guide.

Preparing the Soil Layer

While not as exciting as choosing plants and decorative containers or planning a landscaped garden to serve as a room accent, the soil layer deserves some attention. Consider the function of the soil layer in a miniature garden: it supports the plants and their root systems; it provides necessary plant nutrients for normal plant growth; and it permits adequate drainage, ridding the garden of excess moisture and insuring a thriving garden.

A good soil layer consists of potting mix, charcoal, and drainage material for a container without a drainage hole. A layer of sphagnum moss is optional. If your container has a drainage hole, adding some charcoal to the potting mix is an additional safeguard. The purpose of the charcoal is to keep the potting mix "sweet."

Use a sterilized, commercial potting mix for the soil itself. This comes in various sized packages so you buy only the amount you need at the time. Since the potting mix is sterilized, it contains no pests, weed seeds, or soil diseases. No additional nutrients are needed, since rapid growth is not a desirable

If you want an unusual and unique container for your miniature garden, make it yourself. The containers pictured require no special techniques or expensive equipment, and the firing is done by a professional.

Work out the pot design before you begin. You can work freehand or use a cardboard pattern. Pots shrink about 20% when fired, so make the pot larger than the finished size you desire.

Different kinds of moist clays are available in various-sized packages; ask the dealer about the clays and their characteristics. To purchase clay and have pots fired, look in the yellow pages of your telephone directory under "Ceramic Equipment Supplies."

Creating containers from moist clay slabs involves a technique similar to that of rolling out pie crust. To keep the clay moist and malleable, be sure to close the bag tightly.

To make a pot, cut off a piece of clay with a taut length of wire. Roll clay out on canvas or the back of oilcloth; this makes a good nonstick surface. Use ⅜-inch thick slats to support the roller and insure a uniformly thick slab (see picture 1). Repeat this technique for all slabs needed. Cut slab edges with a potter's fettling knife or other knife; use wood slats as a straightedge.

To connect slabs, score all edges to be joined with a needle, then paint liberally with slip (see pictures 2,3). (Slip is glue that holds sides together. Firing makes slip and clay one unit.) To make slip, mix clay with water until it resembles thick cream. Decorative strips of clay or strips to form container base are attached the same way. Smooth joints and edges with a damp sponge or fingertips.

To incise a design, use a pencil (see picture 4), a fork, crumpled foil, fingers, or any other implement to achieve the final appearance. Be sure to practice the design on extra clay first.

If you are interrupted, keep the pot moist by covering with a damp cloth or plastic. Moisten any stiffened edges when you return.

To make a drainage hole, wait until clay begins to stiffen but isn't really hard. Then twirl a knife tip through the pot bottom.

Dry the pot thoroughly in a spot away from drafts and sunlight. Handle it with care, for dried pots are brittle.

After firing—called a bisque or biscuit firing—your pot will be ready to plant.

1. ROLL OUT CLAY on a non-stick surface; use slats to support roller, insure uniform thickness.

2. SCORE EDGES to be joined with a needle; paint scored areas with liberal amounts of slip.

3. JOIN PIECES with scored edges together; press firmly. Slip, clay will harden when fired.

4. INCISE PATTERN with any sharp instrument. Be sure to practice pattern on scrap clay first.

OTHER POTS TO MAKE: (A) Clay strips are draped over a plastic bowl to form a hang-ing garden. (B) Three round sections are stacked on their edges, and decorated by raking with a plastic fork. (C) Two strips, the upper pierced and folded while still soft, form pot that can also hang. (D) Decorative strip is fastened to pot with slip, raked with a fork. (E) Corners of this planter box are pinched, decoration is carved and stamped. (F) Slabs are raked, then design incised with a pencil (see picture 4, opposite). (G) Edges are shaped, then stippled with crumpled aluminum foil. (H) Coils of clay are molded with fingers.

PLASTIC OR PAPER CUP serves as a tool for adding small pebbles or parts of the soil layer to the garden.

USE A CHOPSTICK, dowel, or stick to help arrange the various garden accents in the landscape design.

trait for plants in small gardens. If you wish to make your own potting mix, follow the instructions given on page 11.

Specialty plants such as cactus and succulents, orchids, bromeliads, and African violets require special potting mixes. Most nurseries or garden supply centers that sell these plants will also sell pre-packaged soil mixes specially formulated for the plants' individual needs. Soil preferences of many plants are listed in the Plant Selection Guide, pages 44-79.

Next comes a layer of activated charcoal bits. Its purpose in the garden is to absorb the noxious by-products created in decaying matter in the soil, keeping the mix "sweet." If you do not include a drainage layer, some charcoal should be included in the potting mix. Charcoal is usually available in small quantities in nurseries and garden supply centers; aquarium supply stores are another possible source.

If your container has no drainage hole, include a drainage layer. The drainage material can consist of crushed rocks, pebbles, small pieces of lava or "feather rock," or even broken bits of clay pots. This layer is important to the garden since it holds excess moisture away from the soil layer. It also keeps the plant roots from sitting in soggy soil and permits the roots to obtain oxygen.

A layer of sphagnum moss between the potting mix and the charcoal/drainage layers, while not necessary, serves as a barrier. It prevents the potting mix from sifting down into the layers of charcoal and drainage, and since the moss is composed of organic material, it can be beneficial to the soil. Sphagnum moss is usually purchased in dried form; it can be found in nurseries and garden supply centers.

PLANTING THE MINIATURE GARDEN

Bring together the plants, container, basic landscape design, various elements of the soil layer, and necessary planting tools ready to use. Be sure to allow yourself enough time to complete the planting without rushing. With proper preparation, planting a miniature garden can be a pleasurable project.

Container Preparation

A clean container helps start the garden properly. Wash it in warm, soapy water, rinsing it thoroughly; soap film is not healthy for plants. Dry the container and allow it to sit for an hour or so before planting.

If you use an ammonia-based cleaner, be sure to air the container for several hours, or overnight.

Tools

While a spade, hoe, and rake are ideal tools for backyard planting and maintenance, tools for the miniature garden need to be somewhat less cumbersome. Yet both sets of tools perform similar tasks. You will need implements to dig holes, arrange the landscape, tamp soil around plants, and arrange any decorative elements to be included.

No expensive equipment is necessary. Almost any implement that can perform the required tasks can be used. A kitchen spoon or a small garden trowel can add the potting mix, charcoal, and drainage material. Chopsticks, a small bamboo pole, and doweling can help arrange various garden elements. The most useful tools are your own two hands; they are flexible, easy to manipulate, and cleanup presents no problem.

Watering the planted garden requires special tools. An atomizer or bulb-shaped sprayer (both are pictured on page 12) works best. Both sprayers create a fine mist that disperses the moisture evenly throughout the garden and also creates some humidity.

Cactus and succulent gardens are an exception. They need less frequent waterings and little humidity. Water them with a more conventional watering can or pitcher.

Pruning an established garden can be accomplished by pinching off the offending stem or leaves with your fingers. More inaccessible areas can be reached with a small pair of scissors.

Adding the Soil Layer

The drainage material, charcoal, and potting mix form the medium in which the plants will live and grow. The soil layer needs to be at least 3 inches deep to establish a viable garden. Less soil depth may create problems later.

The drainage material goes in first. (If your container has a drainage hole, partially cover the opening with a piece of broken clay pot or a few pebbles to keep the soil layers from sifting out; no other drainage material is needed.) Whether your drainage material consists of small pebbles, lava or broken clay pots, cover the container bottom to a depth of about ½ to 1 inch.

Next, add a thin layer of activated charcoal. Use enough charcoal to completely cover the drainage material; or add it to the potting mix.

If you plan to use a layer of sphagnum moss, prepare it ahead of time. Its purpose is to prevent any of the potting mix from mixing with the drainage material. Sphagnum moss is usually purchased in dried form. To prepare it, soak it in water overnight, then squeeze out any excess moisture the next day. Spread the moss over the charcoal/drainage layer in a thin, cohesive sheet.

Last, add the commercial potting mix. You should have a layer of at least 2 inches, enough to adequately support the plants and their root systems.

ELIMINATING PESTS

Although gopher excavations in your lawn or deer munching on your prize roses are pest problems miniature or terrarium gardeners need not worry about, the pests you will encounter can be just as difficult to eliminate, and as disastrous to plants.

Prevention is the best way to control pests and diseases on indoor plants. Carefully examine plants before you buy them, especially the undersides of the leaves where most pests work. Then plant the garden in clean containers and sterilized soil. Washing leaves with lukewarm water and a small amount of soap flakes and checking frequently for signs of poor health should help prevent pest infestations.

If you do see signs of insects, try picking the insects off or washing the leaves with a soap and water solution. Swabbing with alcohol and then rinsing with water can also be effective. If all this fails, here is a list of some common insects and their controls. When spraying plants, screen the unaffected plants in a dish garden with a piece of cardboard, or dip the individual plants in the insecticide. Always take the container outdoors to spray.

Ants feed on the honeydew secretions of aphids, mealybugs, and scale insects. They may injure roots or carry away seedlings. Use commercial ant sprays directly on bugs, or remove them by hand.

Aphids suck plant juices which causes poor growth, stunted plants, or curled, distorted leaves. Secretions form base for growth of sooty mold. Use soap solution, pyrethrum, rotenone.

Mealybugs. Sucking stunts or kills plants. Black mold grows on honeydew secretions. Swab with alcohol or spray with petroleum oils.

Scale. Many kinds, usually brown or gray. Suck plant juices resulting in stunted growth. Honeydew attracts ants. Use soap solution, lime sulfur, petroleum oils.

Spider Mites. Can only be seen when many together. Flat, oval, usually red. Leaves may yellow, die, and drop off. Plant growth stunted. Use soap solution, lime sulfur, dusting sulfur, petroleum oils.

Thrips. Fast moving. Barely visible. Feed on and distort foliage. Use pyrethrum, rotenone, petroleum oils.

Whiteflies. Very small, common pests with white, wedge-shaped wings. Flutter around when plant is disturbed. Young attach to and feed on underside of leaves. Leaves turn pale, surfaces covered with honeydew, sooty mold may develop. Use pyrethrum, rotenone, petroleum oils.

FLORISTS' DISH GARDENS combine interesting variety of plants with similar growth requirements. Unusual containers add to appearance. Plants are: (Left) Kalanchoe blossfeldiana; (Center) Podocarpus macrophyllus, Asparagus setaceus, Hedera helix 'Glacier', Asplenium; (Right) Dizygotheca elegantissima, Pilea depressa, Pilea microphylla, Saxifraga sarmentosa, Peperomia 'Astrid'.

Any landscaping, such as a hill or slope, should be formed with additional potting mix.

Planting the Garden

With the soil layer established, planting can begin. If your design includes an inanimate object, such as an unusual rock or a twisted length of driftwood for the garden's focal point, place it first. The plants can then be worked around it.

The easiest method of planting is to begin with the tallest plants first. They are usually placed in or near the center of the landscape design. Dig a hole where the plant is to be located. To remove the plant from its nursery container, rap it firmly against your working counter to dislodge the soil. Cover the soil surface with your fingers (see picture on page 14,

lower right-hand corner), and shake off excess soil, leaving intact the soil clinging to the root ball. Roll the root ball in paper or cloth toweling to form a soil core (see pictures on page 18). Place the core in the prepared hole and carefully tamp the plant down.

Plant the remaining plants in the same manner. After the tallest plants are set, fix the medium-sized plants, then the ground covers. It's easiest to plant from the center out. After all the plants are firmly established, any final garden accents—such as a pebble border—can be placed.

Watering the Garden

Once the garden planting is finished, give the garden its initial watering. Using an atomizer or bulb-

ARTIFICIAL LIGHTING

When the ideal location for your terrarium or miniature garden is away from a good light source, artificial light may be the answer. Plants can also benefit from a combination of natural and artificial light during the short, gray days of winter.

Special fluorescent tubes have been developed to simulate actual sunlight rays and are used to stimulate plants to bloom, produce fruit, and set seeds; these cost more than regular fluorescents.

Plain fluorescent lights can supply sufficient light for plant growth. They can also be used in combination with the less expensive incandescent bulbs. Incandescent lights should not be used alone; they are not strong enough in the red and blue color bands that plants need and they generate too much heat for tender plants.

Whether you buy a lighting unit or make one, provide adjustable height to allow for plant growth and different-sized containers. Start with the tubes 6 to 12 inches above the foliage. If the foliage bunches together unnaturally, plants are receiving too much light. If they become leggy, more light is needed. Fluorescent lighting will not harm plants, so the lights may be set as close as needed for normal plant growth.

If you are making your own fixture, provide a white or foil reflector to direct light onto plants. When placing plants under it, remember the light at the center of the tube is strongest. Several fluorescent tubes placed side by side are best for plants; one tube alone will not support plant life that depends solely on this light. A standard amount of light for all plants is 15 to 20 watts of light for every square foot of growing surface.

Many plants need a period of darkness every 24 hours. Most foliage plants require 10 to 12 hours of light a day; flowering plants need 16. A regular schedule is important to healthy growth. An inexpensive automatic timer can be used to regulate the lights.

When black rings are visible at tube ends, replace them; six months is the average tube life for maximum light output. Preheat tubes are less expensive and last longer than rapid start tubes.

TABLE-TOP UNIT adjusts to various heights. It lights both a miniature garden and plants in pots.

THREE-TIER UNIT provides fluorescent lights with ample room for many containers, plants.

SUCCULENTS CONTRAST in color, form. Plants are Ophiopogon planiscapus and Sedum spathulifolium.

TINY BONSAI POTS planted with small succulents make inexpensive gifts. Plants are multi-colored sedum.

shaped sprayer, completely soak the potting mix (test the soil with your finger to check water penetration).

A word about the water you use: whether you prefer to use tap water, bottled water, or distilled water, allow it to sit overnight to bring it to room temperature. Cold water may be harmful. If you feel your tap water contains too many chemicals or salts, bottled or distilled water will be preferable. Never use softened water.

Further garden care is discussed in the following section.

MAINTAINING THE MINIATURE GARDEN

To keep a miniature garden looking its best, proper maintenance is essential. Frequent checks of moisture levels, watering the garden if moisture level is low, and occasional pruning to retain the garden's shape are most important.

Other garden maintenance includes replacing plants and eradicating pests or plant disease. Replacing a plant is recommended if it cannot be pruned back into the landscape design or if a plant becomes sickly or dies. The alternative is replanting the entire garden. Keeping pests and plant disease under control will prolong the life of your miniature garden.

Watering

All plants need water to survive, but never too much. A saturated potting mix withholds needed oxygen from a plant's roots, causing them to "drown" in the excess moisture. Knowing when to water plants and adding only the necessary amount will keep your garden thriving.

The best way to avoid overwatering is to familiarize yourself with each plant's preferences. (Preferred moisture level is one of the points to consider when selecting compatible plants for a miniature garden. See page 33.) These preferences are listed for many plants in the Plant Selection Guide, pages 44-79.

Testing the soil for the amount of moisture present is a method of determining whether to water or not. Feel the soil with your finger; if the potting mix is dry to a depth of ½ to 1 inch, add water. If the mix is still damp, keep checking periodically about every 3 days.

Use the atomizer or bulb-shaped sprayer to water the garden (sprayers are pictured on page 12). In addition to normal waterings, spray the plant leaves occasionally; this creates some humidity and helps dust the leaves. A discussion concerning the water to be used is on page 38.

Be especially careful when watering gardens without drainage holes, for excess water has no means of escape.

A miniature garden planted with cactus and/or succulents is an exception to watering rules. Most dislike humidity and prefer to dry out completely before being rewatered. Cactus and succulent gardens are discussed further on page 41.

If you're unsure of whether a garden needs water or not, hold off. Plants that need water will begin to droop or show other signs of thirst. Overwatering is the greatest danger a miniature garden can face.

CACTUS & SUCCULENTS

Cactus and succulents with their wide spectrum of shapes, patterns, and colors create interesting dish gardens. Since they grow slowly and thrive in average house temperatures and humidity, cactus and succulents are especially well suited for small gardens. Although they can often survive neglect, desert gardens do look better with a minimum of care.

Use your imagination when selecting a container that will suit the character of the plants; be sure it is deep enough to hold at least 4 inches of soil. If the container does not have drainage holes, cover the bottom with drainage material. Charcoal added to the potting mix will keep it sweet. Soil should not be pure sand. For succulents use equal parts loam, leaf mold, and sand. For cactus add more sand and some gravel.

After planting, wait several days before watering, and then keep moisture sparse for a few weeks. After that, dig into the soil to test for dryness. If water is needed, soak thoroughly. Water again only when soil is completely dry. Your plants will respond if you use tepid water and withhold moisture on cold gray days.

Succulents and cactus achieve the richest colors and most profuse bloom in full sun. They survive in less than maximum light but colors will diminish. Turn plants occasionally to distribute light evenly except when blooming. Water more during bud and bloom period; do not disturb by moving.

Cactus and succulents must rest, usually in the winter when growth will stop or slow down. Do not force growth at this time. Cut down on watering; give just enough to keep soil barely moist, store plant in a cool place, about 50°, and give some light. This period can last from a month to several months and is essential for good health.

During the remainder of the year, cactus and succulents prefer a daytime temperature of 75°, cooler at night. Protect them if temperature drops below 45°. The average humidity in a house is sufficient. Some air circulation is needed, but drafts can be harmful

Here is a small sampling of cactus and succulents for miniature gardens:

Astrophytum (star cactus). Tiny round cacti with geometric patterns on surface. Yellow flower blooms annually on top of plant. From Mexico. *A. asterias* is sometimes called "sand dollar" for its appearance; *A. myriostigma* is called "bishop's cap."

Crassula. Succulents from South Africa. Some interesting miniatures are C. 'Morgan's Pink', a 4-inch hybrid; *C. pyramidalis*, closely packed leaves form bizarre shapes; *C. schmidtii*, long, slender gray-green leaves; *C. teres;* tightly packed column of pale green leaves.

Echeveria. Succulents from the Americas with broad fleshy leaves forming rosettes. Bell-shaped flowers are usually pink, red, and yellow. Includes *E. elegans,* known as Hen and Chicks. A clustering rosette of light blue-green leaves frosted white. *E. pulvinata* has leaves densely covered with white hairs.

Echinocereus. Low globular cacti with highly ornamental spines. Many small species including *E. melanocentrus*, a dark green globe with large red flowers.

Echinopsis (Easter lily cactus, sea urchin cactus). Small cylindrical or globular cactus from South America. Definite vertical ribs. Long-tubed flowers.

Kalanchoe. A succulent with many shapes. *K. blossfeldiana* has dark green leaves edged with red, with red flowers. 'Tom Thumb' variety grows to 6 inches. *K. fedtschenkoi marginata* is called Aurora Borealis Plant for the margins of blue-green leaves which turn pink in the sun. *K. tomentosa* is named Panda Plant for its brown markings on light green furry leaves.

Lithops (living rocks, pebble plants). Succulents disguised as pebbles with a fissure across the middle from which flowers and new leaves emerge. All grow to about 1 inch.

Mammillaria. Huge genus of small, cylindrical or globe-shaped cacti, either single-stemmed or clustered. Covered with bristles. Small flowers arranged in a circle near the top of plant. Includes those called powder puff cactus, bird's-nest cactus, snowball pincushion.

Notocactus. Small globes with bristly, often colored, spines. Cactus from South America. Flowers yellow or purple-red.

Opuntia. Many forms of this cactus. Those with flat, broad joints are called prickly pears; those with cylindrical joints called chollas. Showy flowers in yellow, orange, or red. Several small forms include *O. microdasys* or bunny ears, flat oval pods with tufts of hair.

Sedum. Stonecrop. Trailing and upright succulents. Very tough but dainty looking plants, many with tiny flowers in clusters. Dwarf species include *S. dasyphyllum*, blue-green, closely packed leaves; stems to 2 inches; *S. multiceps*, shaped like a tiny tree; *S. pachyphyllum*, red-tipped cylindrical leaves to 4 inches; *S. stahlii* called coral beads for roundish red leaves closely set on branching stems.

Sempervivum (houseleek). Tightly packed rosettes of leaves with little offsets and star-shaped flowers in clusters. *S. arachnoideum*, called cobweb houseleek for the fine hairs joining tiny gray-green rosettes; *S. tectorum*, Hen and Chickens, rosettes have red-brown tipped leaves.

Pruning

Once a garden begins to grow, pruning will be necessary to keep the original landscape design intact. Trim each plant as soon as it outgrows its spot. Waiting to prune the garden until a number of plants need trimming could prove disastrous. Some plants may grow so rapidly or become so misshapen that even radical pruning cannot restore them. Replacing them with a new plant is the only solution (see below).

The best method of pruning is to snap or pinch off the overgrown appendages with your fingers. If the branch or leaf is difficult to reach, a pair of scissors or a small knife can accomplish the task. Remove dead leaves and spent blossoms in the same manner.

Replacing Plants

Occasionally, a miniature garden can use some revamping. Many factors can create the need for a new plant: plants that outgrow the landscape and cannot be reshaped by pruning; an ailing or dead plant that cannot be restored to health; or a pest-infested plant that endangers the rest of the garden.

Once a problem plant is recognized, replace it immediately. Plant diseases or pests can quickly spread to the rest of the plants, and an overgrown plant may crowd the rest and destroy the design completely.

To replace the offending plant, carefully dig it out with a spoon or trowel. If it merely outgrew its spot in the garden, repot it as a house plant. A diseased or pest-infested plant should be destroyed.

Remove the new plant from its nursery pot and form a soil core around the root ball as shown on page 18. Place the plant in the hole and tamp it down. Water the garden if necessary. The new plant should blend into its surrounding landscape in a

ATOMIZER-TYPE SPRAYER covers plant leaves with a fine mist; spray cleans leaves, and raises humidity.

short time and restore your miniature garden to its previous glory.

Do not expect a miniature garden to last forever. If too many plants become misshapen or disease or pest infestation is widespread, the best solution is to replant the entire garden.

Controlling Pests

Any exposed garden is vulnerable to insect attacks, and gardens planted in semi-open or flat dish containers are no exception. Like your miniature garden, the pests it attracts will be small ones, but small in size only. These tiny creatures can be just as tenacious and destructive as any pests found in your backyard.

Pest problems manifest themselves in various ways: plants suddenly droop or die while the rest of the garden continues to flourish; leaves begin to curl or leaf edges are chewed; or the pests themselves can be seen crawling around the landscape. Inspect the garden periodically for any sign of pests or pest damage. If they aren't visible but plant damage is, some sleuthing may be necessary to uncover the culprits.

First, identify the pest itself. A special interest column on page 37 describes many common pests as well as the best methods of eradicating them. Once you know which pest is devastating the garden, you can eliminate it.

Treating Plant Diseases

To safeguard your miniature garden against plant disease, buy only healthy plants. Most other plant problems you will encounter are created by improper growing conditions.

Carefully inspect plants before you purchase them. Avoid plants that have yellow or pale-colored leaves, brown leaf edges, leggy or atypical growth, or are pot bound (if roots can be seen growing through the drainage hole in the container bottom or on or near the soil surface, the plant is pot bound). Planting healthy plants gives your miniature garden a proper start.

Most other diseases or plant problems are created by improper growing conditions. Crown or root rot is usually caused by poor drainage and overwatering. Loss of leaves may be caused by low humidity. Other problems may stem from too little light, too much light, too much fertilizer, or too little water. Be sure the plants in your miniature garden have the growing conditions they prefer. Individual plant requirements are listed in the Plant Selection Guide, pages 44-79.

Healthy plants maintained in their preferred environment will extend the lifetime of your miniature garden.

ROUNDED CLAY CONTAINER *echoes barrel shapes of cactus. Rugged rock is a desertlike accent.*

TINY FOREST GARDEN *is planted in wooden box. Driftwood acts as background for woodland plants.*

LIVING ROCK SUCCULENTS *are hard to distinguish from the real stones used as garden accents. Flat, glazed ceramic dish does not detract from the unusual planting.*

SELECTING PLANTS *requires advance planning. Many nurseries (above) have special sections of house plants in small pots. Specialty nurseries (right) have large areas devoted to plant groups such as cactus and succulents.*

Plant Selection Guide

The plants selected for inclusion in this guide are suited to the growing conditions offered by terrariums, semi-open containers, and/or dish gardens. This guide is a basic one, offering the most common plants to start your experimentation. Most can be bought at a nursery or florist shop in 2-inch nursery pots and are commonly grouped as "House Plants." Many of the plants are pictured to help you in locating them.

Plants are listed alphabetically by both their botanical (in italic type) and common names. The common names will direct you to the botanical name, where you will also find a description of the plant's appearance, its growth requirements, and varieties that are also suitable for miniature gardens or terrariums. Symbols following each plant show which container or containers are best for the plant:

⬭ — a terrarium or bottle garden

⬭ — a semi-open container

⬭ — a flat, dish-type container

Plants can adapt to other growing conditions, but the suggested containers will provide the ideal environment. Plants that love high humidity and constant moisture will do best in terrariums or bottle gardens. Those that prefer less water and lower humidity will thrive in semi-open containers. Plants that need to dry out between waterings are best suited for dish gardens. If plants outgrow their diminutive gardens, enjoy them potted individually.

Aaron's beard (See *Saxifraga sarmentosa*).

Acorus gramineus variegatus (miniature sweet flag; Japanese sweet flag). A grass-like plant with green and white foliage. This native of Japan likes lots of water, medium to bright light, standard potting mix, high humidity, and room temperatures around 55°. Plants should not touch container sides. See photo, page 46.

A. g. pusillus. A dwarf variety that grows to 6 inches.

Adiantum (maidenhair fern). Of the hundreds of species, most will do well in terrariums. Wiry, black stems hold lacy fronds with bright green leaflets. Mostly native to the tropics, these ferns require shade, ample moisture, potting mix rich in humus, high humidity, and prefer temperatures below 65°. Mature fronds will occasionally die back but new ones soon appear. Best in accessible containers, since dead fronds will require pruning. One of the more difficult ferns to grow. See photo, page 46.

African violet (See *Saintpaulia*).

Aglaonema. Graceful oblong leaves embellish this tropical plant. Adaptable to poor light and low moisture; variegated foliage requires brighter light. Plant in an accessible container for pruning. All plants need standard potting mix, warm temperatures, and humidity over 30%. See photos, page 46.

A. commutatum. Leaves deep green with pale green markings. Variety 'White Rajah' has white markings.

A. modestum. Chinese evergreen. Shiny dark green leaves.

A. treubii. Bluish-green leaves marked with silver. Plant grows to 10 inches.

ACORUS GRAMINEUS VARIEGATUS

ADIANTUM

AGLAONEMA COMMUTATUM

AGLAONEMA TREUBII

ARDISIA CRENATA

ASPARAGUS SETACEUS

Ajuga reptans (carpet bugle, bugle weed). Dark green leaves form a mat on plant. Use as a ground cover. Varieties with purplish or bronze leaves give best color in bright light; blue flowers appear on spikes. Plants require good drainage and are subject to rot and fungus diseases.

Alternanthera bettzickiana (Joseph's coat). Colorful plant with spoon-shaped leaves in mixtures of rose, red, purple, and green. Grows to 16 inches but can be kept compact by pruning; plant in accessible containers. A native of Brazil, this plant thrives in bright light and warm temperatures. Plant in standard potting mix and keep moist.

Aluminum plant (See *Pilea cadierei*).

Anthurium scherzerianum (flamingo flower; pigtail plant). This dwarf form of the popular exotic house plant is more compact and grows slowly to 2 feet. The waxy flowerlike bracts vary in color from deep red through salmon to white. These natives of tropical American jungles need a great deal of humidity, even moisture, and high temperatures (80-90° is best, but plants can tolerate less). Growth stops if temperature drops below 65°. Thrives in potting mix rich in humus and partial shade.

Aphelandra squarrosa. This showy plant has dark

ASPARAGUS DENSIFLORUS 'SPRENGERI'

ASPLENIUM BULBIFERUM

ASPLENIUM NIDUS

green waxy leaves with white veins and showy flower clusters. Native to Mexico and South America. Plant requires diffused light, humidity over 50%, and temperatures from 50 to 70°. With a tendency to grow leggy, plants are normally pruned to stay 12 to 18 inches; plant in accessible containers. The variety 'Louisae' is best known; 'Brockfield' grows more compactly with broader leaves; 'Dania' is most compact.

Aralia elegantissima (See *Dizygotheca elegantissima*).

Ardisia crenata, also known as A. *crenulata*, A. *crispa*; (coral berry). A native of China and Malaya with long, shiny dark green leaves. With adequate growing space, plant may produce scarlet berries. Thrives in standard potting mix, light shade, ample water, and high humidity. Grows slowly to 18 inches. See photo, page 47.

Artillery plant (See *Pilea microphylla*).

Asparagus, ornamental (asparagus fern). The species are not true ferns but have the same feathery qualities. Thrive in standard potting mix with peat moss or ground bark added. Provide adequate drainage. Leaves will turn yellow in inadequate light. Plants like average house temperatures but do not need as much humidity as a true fern. These fast-growing plants are best in accessible containers. Red spider mites are common pests. See photos, pages 47, 52.

A. asparagoides myrtifolius (baby smilax). Has broad, glossy "leaves."

A. densiflorus 'Myeri' (A. *meyeri*). Called foxtail asparagus fern for its stiff upright stems densely covered with tiny needles.

A. d. 'Sprengeri' (A. *sprengeri*). Also hardy but with drooping stems.

A. falcatus (sickle-thorn asparagus). Has glossy leaves.

A. setaceus, A. plumosus. This hardy plant has a delicate appearance. A dwarf version is called 'Nanus.'

Aspidistra elatior, also A. *lurida*; (cast-iron plant). An extremely sturdy plant with tough, glossy, dark green leaf blades. Although tolerant of a variety of conditions, it prefers high humidity, cool temperatures, and a standard potting mix. Light can range from dark shade to filtered sun. The variegated form has leaves striped with white. Leaves lose their variegation if planted in soil that is too rich. For large containers only.

Asplenium (spleenwort). A large genus of graceful but hardy ferns. Plants need high humidity but have a tendency to turn brown in winter if humidity is excessive. Plant in a moisture-retaining potting mix. See photos, left.

A. bulbiferum (mother fern). Native to Malaya, New Zealand. Tolerates a wide range of indoor temperatures.

BEGONIA

BEGONIA

A. *nidus* (bird's nest fern). Solid, pale green fronds that unfurl from heart of plant.

Aucuba japonica (Japanese aucuba). Shrub with shiny, oval green leaves. It requires high humidity, cool temperatures, and indirect sunlight. Use standard potting mix and keep moist. Prune to keep small.

A. *j.* 'Crotonifolia'. Leaves are heavily splashed with white and gold splotches. Use in large containers only.

A. *j.* 'Variegata' (gold dust plant). Yellow specks on green leaves.

Australian silk oak (See *Grevillea robusta*).

Baby smilax (See *Asparagus asparagoides myrtifolius*).

Baby's tears (See *Soleirolia soleirolii*, *Pilea depressa*, and *Peperomia rotundifolia*).

Ball fern (See *Davallia mariesii*).

Balsam (See *Impatiens walleriana*).

Basket selaginella (See *Selaginella apus*).

Bead plant (See *Nertera granadensis*).

Begonia. About 1,000 species. Tuberous, rhizomatous, bulbous, or fibrous-rooted. Begonias tend to sprawl and need heavy pruning; try dwarf varieties for a terrarium or dish garden. Rich, porous soil should be kept moist, but overly wet conditions may

BEGONIA

BROMELIAD-AECHMEA CHANTINII

cause stem rot. Most species prefer filtered light and a temperature range from 75° to 85°. See photos, page 49.

Bird's nest fern (See *Asplenium*).
Bleeding heart (See *Clerodendrum thomsoniae*).
Bloodleaf (See *Iresine herbstii*).
Boston fern (See *Nephrolepis*).
Bowstring hemp (See *Sansevieria trifasciata*).
Box-leaf euonymus (See *Euonymus japonica microphylla*).
Boxwood (See *Buxus microphylla japonica*).
Brake (See *Pteris*).
Brilliant star (See *Kalanchoe blossfeldiana*).
Bromeliad. A large family of mostly stemless plants with broad or grasslike leaves. Grow well in the dry atmosphere of a house and will thrive in any fast-draining potting mix. Prefer temperatures between 50° to 70°, filtered, bright light. *Tillandsia ionantha* grows to 4 inches. Look also for small forms of *Aechmea, Billbergia, Cryptanthus,* and *Uriesia*. See photos, left.
Bugle weed (See *Ajuga reptans*).
Busy Lizzie (See *Impatiens walleriana*).
Button fern (See *Pellaea rotundifolia*).
Buxus microphylla japonica (Japanese boxwood). A miniature, small-leafed, slow-growing shrub with smooth, firm, rich green foliage. Likes full sun, cool

BROMELIAD-CRYPTANTHUS ZONATUS 'ZEBRINUS'

BUXUS MICROPHYLLA JAPONICA

temperatures, standard potting mix, and average moisture. See photo, page 50.

B. m. koreana (Korean boxwood). Slower growing and smaller than Japanese boxwood.

Caladium bicolor (fancy-leafed caladium). Arrow-shaped translucent leaves in red, pink, white, green, and silver, often with a variety of colors on the same leaf. Keep this tropical American plant in partial shade or filtered sun at a temperature from 70° to 80°. Thrives in a mixture of sand and garden loam; keep potting mix on the acid side for best color. Plants should be moist, never soggy. Decrease water when foliage dies back. In about a month, tubers should be lifted from mix and stored at 50° to 60° so plants must be accessible. 'Humboldtii,' is the smallest and daintiest of the genus.

Calathea. Usually called *Maranta* (see page 64), to which they are closely related. Also called peacock plant. Beautifully marked leaves in shades of green, white, and pink. From tropical America or Africa, these plants need a warm, moist atmosphere, with temperatures not below 55°. Plant in standard potting mix with good drainage in filtered sun. See photo, right.

California pitcher plant (See *Darlingtonia californica*).

Callisia elegans (striped inch plant). A creeper with white or yellow striped green leaves with purple underneath. Grows best in indirect sunlight, average house temperatures. Use standard potting mix and keep it moist at all times. Frequent pruning will promote compact growth.

Cape primrose (See *Streptocarpus*).

Carpet bugle (See *Ajuga reptans*).

Cast-iron plant (See *Aspidistra elatior*).

Ceropegia woodii (rosary vine; string of hearts). A fast-growing, succulent vine from South Africa with hanging or trailing stems growing from a tuberous base. Heart-shaped leaves in pairs are dark green marbled with white, rose-colored underneath. Plant in a sandy potting mix with extra humus; water when soil surface is dry; keep in filtered sunlight. Occasionally, the plant may appear to wilt; it is resting, so hold back on water until new growth appears.

Chamaedorea elegans, also *Neanthe bella*. A dwarf species of the parlor palm from Columbia. Single-stemmed, slow-growing plant will tolerate crowded roots and poor light. Graceful, arching fronds of leathery, dark green leaves. Likes average humidity and occasional water. See photo, right.

Chamaeranthemum. Foliage in different colors with veined patterns. Plant in equal parts loam, sand, and peat moss. Likes high humidity, diffused sunlight, even moisture, and average indoor temperatures.

CALATHEA

CHAMAEDOREA ELEGANS

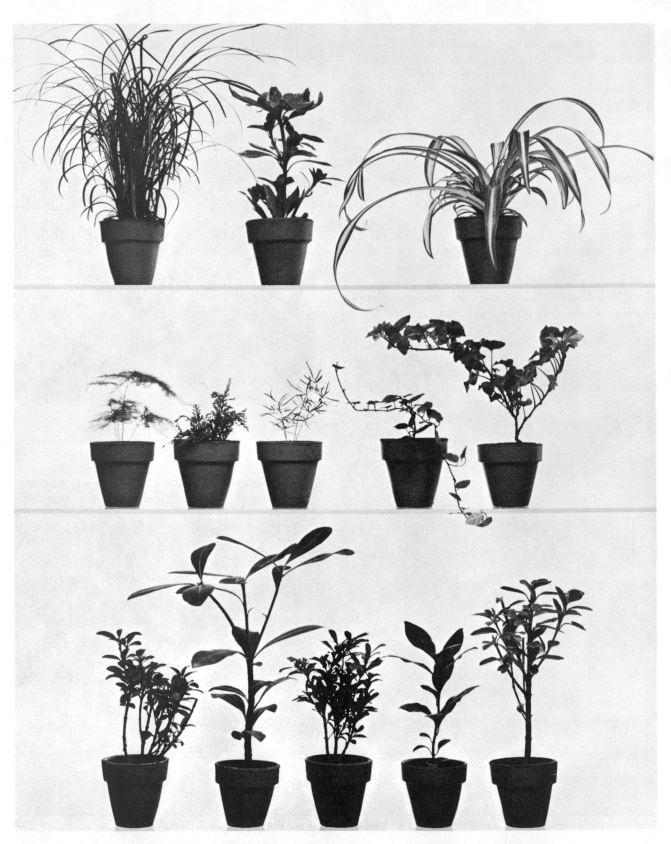

TOP ROW, FROM LEFT: LIRIOPE; PACHYSANDRA TERMINALIS; CHLOROPHYTUM COMOSUM. CENTER: ASPARAGUS SETACEUS; ASPLENIUM BULBIFERUM; ASPARAGUS DENSIFLORUS 'SPRENGERI'; FICUS PUMILA; HEDERA HELIX. BOTTOM: EUONYMUS JAPONICA; PITTOSPORUM TOBIRA; BUXUS; SARCOCOCCA RUSCIFOLIA; EUONYMUS 'SILVER QUEEN'.

C. gaudichaudii. A small creeper from Brazil. Silver-centered dark green leaves.

C. igneum. Suede-like leaves veined in shades of red and yellow.

C. venosum. Leaves mottled with silver.

Chinese evergreen (See *Aglaonema modestum*).

Chlorophytum comosum 'Vittatum' (spider plant). Clumps of grasslike leaves with white or yellow margins. Miniature duplicates of the mother plant are produced at stem ends. Prefers full light, but can tolerate less. Other needs are average house temperatures and average humidity. Plant in standard potting mix and keep moist. Best in large containers or hanging gardens. Chlorophytum is native to Africa. See photo, page 52.

Cissus. A vine with glossy green leaflets, it tends to grow up and around the top of a terrarium. Reddish hairs underneath give leaves bronze overtones. Adaptable to average house temperatures and light conditions, these plants like lots of water. Plant in standard potting mix. Will require pruning to keep compact. See photo, right.

C. antarctica 'Minima' (dwarf kangaroo ivy). Waxy green leaves on a compact plant.

C. rhombifolia. Grape ivy.

C. striata. Called miniature grape ivy.

CISSUS RHOMBIFOLIA

CLERODENDRUM THOMSONIAE

CODIAEUM AUCUBAEFOLIUM

CODIAEUM VARIEGATUM

Clerodendrum thomsoniae (glorybower; bleeding heart). Large vine with long, dark green, shiny, oval leaves; distinctly ribbed, striking red and white flowers. Native to west Africa. Plant in standard potting mix with good drainage; give plenty of water. Likes bright light, average temperatures and 30% humidity. Plant in large, accessible containers. See photo, page 53.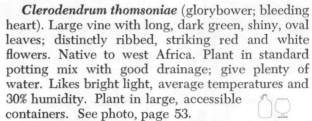

Cobra lily (See *Darlingtonia californica*).

Codiaeum. A tropical plant that needs bright light for best color. Grows to 15 inches in standard potting mix; keep moist but not soggy. Keep temperatures above 70° but allow for some fresh air. See photos, right.

C. aucubaefolium (gold dust plant; gold spot). A bushy plant with bright green, glossy leaves spotted or blotched yellow.

C. variegatum (croton). A plant with glossy leaves in spectacular shades of green, yellow, red, purple, and bronze. Plant in large container only.

Coffea arabica (coffee tree). Glossy dark green leaves are very tender. Plant in standard potting mix with added organic material and keep in filtered light, average house temperatures. Young seedling can be pinched to induce bushiness.

Coffee tree (See *Coffea arabica*).

COLEUS

COLEUS

Coleus. Brilliant multi - colored leaves, often ruffled or scalloped. Colors will lose luster in too much shade or too much sun; plant grows best in light shade or strong indirect light. Thrives in standard potting mix with added humus, perfect drainage, warm temperatures, ample moisture, and some fresh air. See photos, page 54.

Columnea microphylla. Trailing plant from tropical America with tiny coppery leaves. Plant in standard potting mix. Thrives in moist soil, high humidity, and temperatures from 65° to 75°. Prefers semi-sunny to semi-shady light. Good for hanging gardens.

Common spiderwort (See *Tradescantia virginiana*).

Coral berry (See *Ardisia crenata*).

Corkscrew flower (See *Phaseolus caracalla*).

Corn plant (See *Dracaena fragrans*).

Creeping Charlie (See *Pilea nummularifolia*).

Crossandra infundibuliformis. Glossy, dark green, gardenialike foliage. This native of India needs high humidity, good light, and warmth. Plant it in rich potting mix that contains some humus; water frequently. Plant in accessible containers. Crossandra's coral-orange flowers need to be removed when spent.

Croton (See *Codiaeum variegatum*).

Cycas revoluta (Sago palm). Young plants have the airy, lacy appearance of ferns but are related to conifers. Tolerant of many conditions but do best in partial shade, abundant moisture. Grows slowly.

Cymbalaria muralis (Kenilworth ivy). Dainty, trailing, European plant with small, smooth, lobed leaves. Likes a cool garden with moderate light, ample water, and high humidity. Plant in a standard potting mix with peat moss and leaf mold added. See photo, at right.

C. aequitriloba. A miniature with tiny lavender flowers.

Cyperus alternifolius (umbrella plant). This rush-like plant related to papyrus has an umbrella-shaped cluster of leaves on top of a slender stem. It grows best with constant moisture, high humidity, and good light but not full sun. Keep on the cool side. Its use in terrariums and dish gardens is very limited because of its size; use smaller varieties.

C. a. gracilis. A small variety to 2 feet.

C. a. 'Nanus' is a dwarf form.

Cyrtomium falcatum (holly fern). Resembles Christmas holly with its shiny firm-textured foliage. Native to Japan. Demands less humidity than most ferns. Provide medium to bright light, cool to average temperatures, and standard potting mix kept moist. See photo, at right.

Darlingtonia californica (California pitcher plant; cobra lily). Native to Northern California and Ore-

CYMBALARIA MURALIS

CYRTOMIUM FALCATUM

DARLINGTONIA CALIFORNICA

gon, it captures insects in a hooded, red-veined, pitcher-shaped leaf. The insects become food for the plant when decayed. It thrives in sphagnum moss kept constantly moist. Do not use alkaline water—rainwater is the safest. Likes filtered sunlight and cool temperatures. Plant grows to 15 inches. Use in large containers only. See photo, left.

Davallia mariesii (ball fern). The smallest of a group of ferns with creeping furry stems that grow above ground. Grows six to eight inches with green, feathery fronds. Plant in lightweight potting mix and keep moist. Likes shade, cool temperatures, and high humidity.

D. trichomanoides (squirrel's foot fern). Large variety; plant in accessible container.

Devil's backbone (See *Pedilanthus tithymaloides*).

Devil's ivy (See *Rhaphidophora aurea*).

Dionaea muscipula (Venus flytrap). This insect-eating plant does not need flies to survive. It flourishes in a closed garden or terrarium which simulates the humid atmosphere of its native Carolina habitat. Full sun brings out the deep red coloring. Grow in sphagnum moss with a little sand and leaf mold added. Keep constantly moist. Plant grows to 6 inches and prefers cool temperatures (around 60°). See photo, below.

DIONAEA MUSCIPULA

DIZYGOTHECA ELEGANTISSIMA

Dizygotheca elegantissima, also *Aralia elegantissima*; (threadleaf false aralia). Young plant has lacy leaves, dark green above, reddish-colored underneath. Plant in a standard potting mix with good drainage and keep constantly moist but never soggy. Thrives in ample light, not direct sun, and high humidity. Grows slowly. See photo, page 56.

Dracaena. This palmlike plant from west Africa needs frequent pruning. To prune, remove older leaves at base. Tolerates ordinary soil, average light, moisture, and humidity. See photos, this page.

D. fragrans (corn plant). Grows upright with green cornlike leaves. Requires less light than other dracaenas. Variety 'Massangeana' has broad yellow stripe in center of leaf.

D. godseffiana (gold dust plant). Small, slow grower. Dark green leaves irregularly spotted with yellow or white.

D. sanderiana. Grows upright. Resembles a corn plant with white striped leaves.

D. deremensis 'Warneckii'. Deep blue-green leaves with a narrow, white stripe.

Drosera rotundifolia (sundew). Tiny insect-eater with spoon-shaped growth covered with red hairs tipped with a sticky substance. Requires good light

DRACAENA FRAGRANS

DRACAENA GODSEFFIANA

DRACAENA SANDERIANA

EPISCIA CUPREATA

and ample moisture. Plant in mixture of sphagnum moss and loam.

Dryopteris erythrosora (wood fern). One of the few ferns with seasonal color; young fronds are reddish bronze turning to deep green in late spring and summer. Eventually grows too big for most terrariums but maintains a low, compact rosette for one or two growing seasons. Native to China and Japan, it thrives in shade, ample moisture, potting mix rich in humus, and high humidity.

Emerald ripple (See *Peperomia caperata*).

English ivy (See *Hedera helix*).

Episcia cupreata (flame violet; peacock plant). A creeping relative of the African violet with oval velvety leaves in beautiful colors and orange-red blossoms. As with strawberries, new plantlets are formed at runner ends. Plant needs are high humidity, partial shade, ample water, and temperatures from 60° to 75°. Use African violet potting mix. See photos, at left.

***Euonymus japonica* 'Microphylla'** (box-leaf euonymus). Compact, small-leafed version of the outdoor shrub, Japanese euonymus. Plant in standard potting mix. Grow with filtered light and temperatures under 60°. Don't overwater. Prune frequently for indoor use. Yellow variegated (Golden

EPISCIA CUPREATA

EUONYMUS JAPONICA 'MICROPHYLLA'

Queen), and white variegated (silver lining plant) forms are most common. See photos, pages 52, 58.

False holly (See *Osmanthus heterophyllus*).

Fatsia japonica, also *Aralia sieboldii, A. japonica* (Japanese aralia). Tropical plant with glossy, dark green, deeply lobed, fan like leaves. Use young plant and keep pruned. Keep light filtered; foliage yellows with too much sun. Tolerates any soil, prefers temperatures under 70°, ample moisture.

Ferns (See *adiantum, asplenium, cyrtomium, davallia, nephrolepis, pellaea, polystichum, pteris*).

Fern pine (See *Podocarpus gracilior*).

Ficus. Members of the fig family. Thrive in standard potting mix, average room temperatures, indirect sunlight, and average humidity. See photos, pages 52, 59.

F. diversifolia (mistletoe fig). Raindrop shaped, dark green leaves, sometimes stippled tan. A native of Malaya; greenish to yellow fruit is produced continuously. Provide diffused light and more than average water. Prune to keep compact.

F. pumila (F. repens). A rapid climber with tiny, heart-shaped leaves. Will cling to rough surfaces.

F. p. minima. A dwarf creeper.

Fittonia verschaffeltii (mosaic plant; nerve plant). A creeper with dark green leaves laced with veins of red or bright pink. Native to South America. Needs strong diffused light; not suitable for tinted glass. Leaves are not too flexible, so small bottle openings may be a problem. Keep moist and do not let temperature drop below 55°. Plants thrive in high humidity. The variety 'Argyroneura' is veined with white. See photo, at right.

Flame violet (See *Episcia cupreata*).

Flamingo flower (See *Anthurium scherzerianum*).

Foxtail asparagus fern (See *Asparagus densiflorus*).

Freckle face (See *Hypoestes sanguinolenta*).

Geogenanthus undatus (seersucker plant). Silver-striped leaves are rich purple underneath and have a "seersucker" texture. Plant grows to 1 foot; keep pruned. Tropical plant from Peru. Keep humidity high, temperatures warm, and standard potting soil moist but not soggy. Provide filtered light.

Geranium, miniature (See *Pelargonium*).

Glorybower (See *Clerodendrum thomsoniae*).

Gloxinia, miniature (See *Sinningia pusilla*).

Gold dust plant (See *Codiaeum aucubaefolium* and *Dracaena godseffiana*).

Grape ivy (See *Cissus rhombifolia*).

Green carpet plant (See *Herniaria glabra*).

Grevillea robusta (Australian silk oak). A tall, fast-growing tree used when small for its graceful showy fernlike leaves. A native of Australia, it needs

FICUS DIVERSIFOLIA

FITTONIA VERSCHAFFELTII

FROM LEFT: PODOCARPUS MACROPHYLLUS; GREVILLEA ROBUSTA; PODOCARPUS GRACILIOR

GYNURA AURANTIACA

a temperature range of 50° to 65°, filtered sun, and standard potting mix with good drainage. Keep moist but not soggy. Requires frequent pruning to keep compact. See photo, page 60.

Gynura aurantiaca (velvet plant). Dark green lance-shaped, toothed leaves are covered with purple fuzz, giving a velvety appearance. This plant from the East Indies develops best leaf color in strong light. Other needs are standard potting mix with added humus, good drainage, temperatures about 70°, and sufficient moisture at the roots and on the foliage (spray foliage frequently to provide humidity). If plant blooms and an unpleasant odor appears, snap off blossoms. Plant in accessible containers; prune to keep compact. See photo, at left.

Hart's tongue fern (See *Phyllitis scolopendrium*).

Hedera helix (English ivy). Many varieties. Prefers a cool temperature, not over 65°, ample light and moisture. These crawling plants can serve as ground covers, grow up the sides of a container, or spill over the sides. See photos, page 61.

H. h. 'Baltica'. Hardy, has leaves half the size of English ivy with whitish veins that turn purple in

HEDERA HELIX

HEDERA HELIX 'NEEDLEPOINT'

HEDERA HELIX 'FAN'

HEDERA HELIX 'SYLVANIAN'

PLANT SELECTION GUIDE **61**

HOYA CARNOSA

HYPOESTES SANGUINOLENTA

IMPATIENS WALLERIANA

winter. Other miniature-leafed varieties are 'Glacier,' 'Fan,' 'Gold Dust,' 'Maple Leaf,' 'Needlepoint,' 'Hahn's Self-Branching.'

Hedge fern (See *Polystichum*).

Herniaria glabra (green carpet plant; rupture wort). Trailing fine-textured dense ground cover is hardier than selaginellas and will take much abuse. Bright green color turning to bronze in cold climate. Tolerates a variety of conditions but becomes leggy in poor light.

Holly, false (See *Osmanthus heterophyllus*).

Holly fern (See *Cyrtomium falcatum*).

Holly, miniature (See *Malpighia*).

Hoya carnosa (wax plant; wax flower). Thick, waxy green leaves; immature leaves are red. Has large, compact clusters of creamy white flowers. Variegated forms are not as vigorous or hardy as the solid green form. 'Compacta' has crinkled leaves spaced closely on short stem. This plant is semi-dormant in winter, requiring less light and moisture, and a lower temperature. Starting in February, water freely, keep humid, and maintain temperatures about 70°. Likes ample light and a standard potting mix. See photo, above.

H. c. 'Tricolor.' Variegated form of green and white leaves with pink edges.

Hypoestes sanguinolenta (freckle face; pink

polka-dot plant). Irregular pink spots on oval green leaves. Native to Madagascar. Prefers loose potting mix with some peat moss, strong light, even moisture, at least 30% humidity, warm temperatures. If plant dies back, new growth will appear. See photo, page 62.

Impatiens walleriana (balsam, touch-me-not, snapweed, patient Lucy, busy Lizzie). Use dwarf perennial types to add color to well-lit, accessible glass containers. Blooms range in color from scarlet, pink, violet, orange to white. Keep standard potting soil moist; average house temperatures should not become too warm. Humidity over 50% helps avoid red spider mites. See photo, page 62.

Indoor oak (See *Nicodemia diversifolia*).

Iresine herbstii (bloodleaf). Translucent crimson or yellowish leaves and branches grow on this spectacular plant from Brazil. Color can vary greatly; needs good light for best color display. Thrives in standard potting mix, average humidity. Let dry between watering. Growth is bushy with some climbing and trailing; needs pruning to keep compact. See photo, at right.

Ivy (See *Hedera helix*).

Ivy-arum (See *Rhaphidophora aurea*).

Japanese aralia (See *Fatsia japonica*).

Japanese aucuba (See *Aucuba japonica*).

Japanese boxwood (See *Buxus microphylla japonica*).

Japanese privet (See *Ligustrum japonicum*).

Japanese spurge (See *Pachysandra terminalis*).

Japanese sweet flag (See *Acorus gramineus variegatus*).

Joseph's coat (See *Alternanthera*).

Kalanchoe blossfeldiana (brilliant star). Succulent with dark green leaves edged in red. 'Tom Thumb' variety grows to 6 inches. Waxy red blossoms appear annually. After blooms fade, prune tops severely and let plants rest. Prefers full sun to semi-shade, warm temperatures, and sandy potting mix with humus added. Let soil dry between watering. See also page 41. See photo, right.

Kangaroo ivy (See *Cissus antarctica*).

Kenilworth ivy (See *Cymbalaria muralis*).

Korean boxwood (See *Buxus microphylla koreana*).

Leopard lily (See *Sansevieria trifasciata*).

Ligustrum japonicum 'Texanum' (waxleaf privet; Japanese privet; Texas privet). When young, this outdoor shrub will thrive in dish gardens. Give it cool temperatures, direct sunlight, and moist standard potting mix. Prune frequently to keep small.

Liriope and *Ophiopogon* (mondo grass). Both members of the lily family, these plants are similar in appearance. Clumps of grass-like leaves, plain

IRESINE HERBSTII

KALANCHOE BLOSSFELDIANA

LIRIOPE

LIRIOPE

green or variegated. Keep temperature below 72° and humidity over 30%. Use a standard potting mix. Will tolerate light from full sun to shade. See photos, page 52, 64.

O. japonicus. Smallest form is best for dish gardens.

Maidenhair fern (See *Adiantum*).

Malpighia coccigera (miniature holly). Small glossy leaves with spiny margins grow on this tough plant from tropical America. Grow in standard potting mix; let dry between heavy waterings. Needs average light, at least 30% humidity, and temperatures from 55° to 70°. Likes cooler nights. Will require occasional pruning. See photo, page 52.

Maranta leuconeura (prayer plant; rabbit tracks). Large green leaves with paired brown spots. At night, the leaves fold together, resembling hands in prayer. Low, bushy growth makes it a good background plant. Old or straggly leaves will need pruning. Grow in standard potting mix with filtered light, high humidity, and warm temperatures above 65°. See photos, page 65.

M. l. 'Massangeana'. Large leaves with prominent veins and pink spots. Is larger than prayer plant.

Maranta (See also *Calathea*).

Mimosa pudica (sensitive plant). Delicate apple green leaves fold temporarily when touched, quickly recover. This native of Guatemala likes strong light, warmth, high humidity, and moist but not soggy soil. Use standard potting mix.

Ming aralia (See *Polyscias fruticosa* 'Elegans').

Miniature holly (See *Malpighia*).

Mistletoe fig (See *Ficus diversifolia*.)

Mondo grass (See *Liriope* and *Ophiopogon*).

Mosaic plant (See *Fittonia verschaffeltii*).

Moss fern (See Selaginella).

Mother fern (See *Asplenium*).

Mother-in-law's tongue (See *Sansevieria trifasciata*).

Mother-of-thousands (See *Saxifraga sarmentosa*).

Nephrolepis exaltata (sword fern). Stiff erect fronds on ferns which spread by thin runners. Tolerates poor soil and a variety of light and watering conditions. Provide average temperatures and humidity with ample fresh air. Usually too large for small containers. See photo, page 65.

N. e. 'Bostoniense'. Boston fern.

Nertera granadensis (bead plant). Tiny, smooth rounded leaves form a dense green mat. Plant produces beadlike orange fruit. Thrives in light sandy soil, shade, and constant moisture.

Nerve plant (See *Fittonia verschaffeltii*).

Nicodemia diversifolia (indoor oak). Small branching shrub from Madagascar with iridescent oak leaves. Likes bright, indirect light and warm temperatures. Grow in standard potting mix kept barely moist at all times. Prune frequently to keep small. For a bushier appearance, pinch back new growth.

Osmanthus heterophyllus (false holly). A holly-like plant that grows slowly to three feet or more. It thrives in direct sun, cool temperatures, but will tolerate semi-shade and drafts. Keep standard potting mix moist at all times. Prune to keep small.

Oxalis. Cloverlike leaves on a small plant. Many species grow from bulbs or tubers. Leaves fold closed at night. Likes standard potting mix with extra humus, strong light, at least 30% humidity, and temperatures around 60°. Plants are deciduous; use accessible containers. See photo, page 66.

Pachysandra terminalis (Japanese spurge). Palm-like rosettes of rich dark green leaves on plant which spreads by underground runners. 'Silveredge' and 'Variegata' are variegated forms. Prefers acid potting mix rich in humus, plenty of water, and shade. See photo, page 52.

Panamiga, panamigo (See *Pilea involucrata*).

Pandanus (screw pine). Spirally arranged foliage with prickly-edged, spearlike leaves. Many varieties are banded with white or silver. This shrub from the South Pacific will thrive in standard potting mix,

MARANTA LEUCONEURA

MARANTA LEUCONEURA 'MASSANGEANA'

NEPHROLEPIS EXALTATA

OXALIS OREGANA

warmth, bright light, average house temperatures, and high humidity. Water frequently. Use in large containers.

Patient Lucy (See *Impatiens walleriana*).

Peacock plant (See *Calathea; Episcia cupreata*).

Pedilanthus tithymaloides (devil's backbone; redbird cactus). Common names come from strange zigzag stems and small birdlike blossoms in spring. Lance-shaped leaves of this succulent are light green with splashes of red, white, and dark green. 'Nanus' is a dwarf variety. Likes full sun to semi-shade, average temperatures and humidity, a potting mix of equal parts loam, sand, and peat moss, and even moisture. See photo, below.

Pelargonium (geranium). Many compact miniatures with blooms in full range of geranium colors. Plant in mixture of equal parts sand and garden soil and do not allow soil to dry out. Give full sun and temperatures from 60° to 70°. Keep pruned. Humidity should not get too high; allow air to circulate frequently.

Pellaea rotundifolia (button fern; roundleaf fern). A small, rock-loving fern. Round, dark green leaflets are a contrast to normal fern foliage. Requires filtered light, a standard potting mix, good drainage, and high humidity.

Pellionia. Interesting variegated foliage on this trailing plant from tropical Asia. It requires strong light, temperatures from 65° to 75°, high humidity, and ample water at roots.

P. daveauana. Brown leaves with apple green stripes.

P. pulchra (rainbow vine). Patterned leaves with colors of brown, maroon.

Peperomia. A large group of plants with a variety of interesting foliage. Grow in standard potting mix with good drainage, strong filtered light, high humidity, and warmth. Do not overwater. 'Astrid' is a small plant with fleshy leaves. See photos, page 67.

P. caperata ('Emerald ripple'). Three to 4-inch plants with heart shaped leaves, reddish stalks. 'Little Fantasy' is a miniature variety.

P. fosteri. A trailing variety with reddish stems.

P. magnoliaefoliae. Almost round leaves with yellow variegation.

P. metallica. Erect, dark red stems, with narrow waxy leaves of copper with a metallic luster and a silver green band down the middle.

P. obtusifolia. Round leaves. 'Minima' is a miniature form.

P. rotundifolia (baby's tears). Slender trailing stems, tiny leaves.

P. sandersii (watermelon peperomia). Compact plant with silver, curved strips on thick oval leaves.

Periwinkle, dwarf (See *Vinca minor*).

Philodendron oxycardium (*P. cordatum*). Shiny, red-pointed buds uncurl into heart-shaped leaves.

PEDILANTHUS TITHYMALOIDES

PEPEROMIA 'ASTRID'

PEPEROMIA CAPERATA

PEPEROMIA MAGNOLIAEFOLIA

PEPEROMIA SANDERSII

PHILODENDRON OXYCARDIUM

PILEA 'MOON VALLEY'

PILEA 'SILVER TREE'

Climbs or trails. Keep pruned for a compact plant. Grows rapidly in standard potting mix. Adaptable to average temperatures, humidity, and light conditions. Do not overwater. See photo, above left.

Phoenix roebelenii (pigmy date palm). Fine-leafed, small, graceful palm. A native of Laos. Plant in standard potting mix with leaf mold, humus, and decomposed manure added. Needs good light, ample moisture with good drainage, and warmth.

Phyllitis scolopendrium (hart's tongue fern). Unusual fern with glossy, undivided, strap-shaped fronds. Likes moisture, shade, high humidity, and cool temperatures. Many dwarf varieties.

Pick-a-back (See *Tolmiea menziesii*).
Piggy-back plant (See *Tolmiea menziesii*).
Pigmy date palm (See *Phoenix roebelenii*).
Pigtail plant (See *Anthurium scherzerianum*).
Pilea. Juicy-stemmed plant which becomes leggy with too much shade. Plant in standard potting mix with good drainage, keep day temperatures from 75° to 85°, and have moist but not soggy soil. See photos, above, left, page 69.

P. cadierei (aluminum plant). Erect growth with showy, silver-flecked leaves. 'Minima' is a dwarf variety.

PILEA CADIEREI

PILEA DEPRESSA

PILEA INVOLUCRATA

PILEA MICROPHYLLA

PLECTRANTHUS

PLECTRANTHUS COLEOIDES 'MARGINATUS'

P. depressa (baby's tears). Bright, apple green, tiny leaves. Use as a ground cover.

P. involucrata (panamiga; panamigo). Glossy bronze-green leaves with lighter veins. Low spreading growth.

P. microphylla (artillery plant). Tiny, thick, bright green leaves in fernlike sprays. This creeper requires pruning to keep confined.

P. nummulariaefolia (creeping Charlie). A creeping plant with small, round, slightly hairy leaves and a tendency for stems to root at each node. A good ground cover.

Pink polka-dot plant (See *Hypoestes sanguinolenta*).

Pitcher plant (See *Sarracenia*).

Pittosporum tobira. Thick, shiny, leathery leaves are arranged in whorls at the branch tips. Normally used as an outdoor shrub, it is pruned for indoor use. The variegated form is smaller. Light can vary from semi-sunny to semi-shady. Keep temperature below 75° and the humidity over 30%. Plant in standard potting mix; keep evenly moist, never soggy. See photo, page 52.

Plectranthus (Swedish ivy). A trailing plant from Africa with round, thick, often variegated leaves. Needs standard potting mix, average temperatures, moisture, and humidity. Tolerates dim light. Fast growing. See photos, left.

P. australis. Dark green leaves.

P. coleoides **'Marginatus'.** Dark green leaves with white serrated edges.

P. oertendahlii. Apple green leaves with silver veins.

Podocarpus. These trees and shrubs are slow-growing and stay compact if pruned when young. Adaptable to many conditions, they grow best in semi-shade, cool temperatures (below 75°), at least 30% humidity, and standard potting mix kept evenly moist. See photos, pages 60, 71.

P. gracilior (fern pine). Willowy, graceful form.

P. macrophyllus maki (shrubby yew pine). A slow-growing variety that prunes to shape easily.

Polyscias. Several species related to the aralia. Provide ample light but no direct sun, high humidity, standard potting mix, good drainage.

P. filicifolia. Bright green, fernlike leaves.

P. fruticosa **'Elegans'** (Ming aralia). Parsleylike leaves on woody stem.

P. guilfoylei. Coarse, oaklike foliage.

Polystichum (hedge fern). Dark green fronds grow on symmetrical ferns. These hardy plants grow best in a standard potting mix with added humus, shade, ample water, and average indoor temperatures and humidity.

P. tsus-simense. A dwarf variety that grows to 8 inches with leathery, dark green fronds.

Pothos aureus (See *Rhapidophora aurea.*)

Prayer plant (See *Maranta leuconeura*).

Pteris (brake, table fern, ribbon fern, Victoria fern). Small tropical ferns best known for forked and crested green or variegated fronds. There are many tiny varieties with interesting foliage. Prefer semi-shade, cool temperatures, and at least 50% humidity. See photos, below.

P. quadriaurita 'Argyraea' (silver lace). Delicate appearance.

P. ensiformis 'Victoria'. Silvery white fronds edged in dark green.

Rabbit tracks (See *Maranta leuconeura*).

Rainbow vine (See *Pellionia pulchra*).

Redbird cactus (See *Pedilanthus tithymaloides*).

Rex begonia (See *Begonia*).

Rhapidophora aurea, also known as *Scindapsus aureus*, *Pothos aureus* (silver pothos, devil's ivy, ivy-arum). Oval, leathery leaves with pale splotches, similar to philodendron leaves. Climbs or trails. Grow in standard potting soil, good light, ample water, and warmth. See the photo on page 72.

Ribbon fern (See *Pteris*).

Rosa chinensis 'Minima' (miniature rose). These tiny roses that grow to six inches are not just dwarf forms of the larger roses but a separate strain. Almost 100 varieties are available in a wide range of colors. Go to a specialty nursery if not available

PODOCARPUS MACROPHYLLUS

PTERIS QUADRIAURITA 'ARGYRAEA'

PTERIS CRETICA 'ALBO-LINEATA'

RHAPIDOPHORA AUREA

SAINTPAULIA 'DOLLY DIMPLE'

locally. Grow them in any light conditions; they will tolerate some sun. Give them standard potting soil, plenty of moisture at their roots, and a complete fertilizer once a month. They thrive under glass in the high humidity but need daily airings. Aphids and red spider are usual pests; mildew is common too. When blooming, miniature roses need constant maintenance.

Rosary vine (See *Ceropegia woodii*).

Rose, Miniature (See *Rosa chinensis* 'Minima').

Roundleaf fern (See *Pellaea rotundifolia*).

Ruellia makoyana (trailing velvet plant). Low, spreading plant with small, satiny, olive green leaves with purple-red shadings and silvery veins. This plant from Brazil likes high humidity, even moisture, filtered light, and daytime temperatures above 65°. Plant in standard potting mix with extra humus.

Rupture wort (See *Herniaria glabra*).

Sago palm (See *Cycas revoluta*).

Saintpaulia (African violet). A wide variety of interesting leaves on this popular house plant; leaves are fuzzy. Blue, white, purple, and pink blossoms offer color. Buy miniature varieties and new plants that respond better to humidity. Best for semi-open gardens. Use commercial African violet potting mix; fertilize regularly if container has a drainage hole.

SAINTPAULIA 'WINTERGREEN'

SANSEVIERIA TRIFASCIATA

SAXIFRAGA SARMENTOSA

Needs are temperatures from 60° to 75°, lots of diffused light, and moist soil and high humidity but not too much moisture. See photos, page 72.

Sarcococca ruscifolia. A slow-growing plant with glossy, waxy, deep green leaves, densely set. A native of China. Plant in potting mix rich in organic matter. Likes shade. See photo, page 52.

Sansevieria trifasciata (snake plant, bowstring hemp, mother-in-law's tongue). Thick, patterned leaves radiate from base. The variety 'Hahnii' is low growing with brilliantly marked leaves. A tough plant from South Africa, it likes sandy soil, infrequent but thorough waterings. Will thrive in most light situations. Use as a background plant. See photo, above.

Sarracenia (pitcher plant). Leaves form hollow pitchers that trap insects by luring them into the pitchers to get at nectar; similar to *Darlingtonia*. Requires a boggy, acid soil, such as peat moss and sphagnum moss mixed with a little sand. They like filtered light, high humidity, and cool temperatures.

Saxifraga sarmentosa (strawberry begonia, strawberry geranium, Aaron's beard, mother-of-thousands). A creeping plant from China and Japan that forms runners like a strawberry, producing

SAXIFRAGA SARMENTOSA 'TRICOLOR'

SEDUM CONFUSUM

SEDUM RUBROTINCTUM

SEDUM ANGLICUM

new plants at stem ends. Nearly round, fuzzy, white-veined leaves with pink underneath. Use standard potting mix and keep evenly moist. Prefers temperatures under 65°, at least 30% humidity, and filtered light. See photos, page 73.

S. s. 'Tricolor'. Green leaves liberally edged in white.

Scindapsus aureus (See *Rhapidophora*).

Screw pine (See *Pandanus*).

Sedum (stonecrop). This large genus includes a wide variety of succulents from many parts of the world. All have fleshy leaves but vary in size, shape, color, and hardiness. Many well-known species have tiny leaves and trailing stems; others grown upright. See page 41 for culture. Some varieties are pictured above, left, page 75.

Seersucker plant (See *Geogenanthus undatus*).

Selaginella (moss fern, spike moss, sweat plant). This branching mosslike plant is taller and fluffier than real moss. Makes a good ground cover in shady, moist situations where humidity is at least 50%. See photo, page 76.

S. apus, also S. *apoda*, S. *densa* (basket selaginella). Smallest form, about 1 inch.

S. denticulata. Yellow-green in color.

S. Kraussiana. A dwarf with bright green leaves.

S. uncinata. Leaves of iridescent metallic blue green.

SEDUM OAXACANUM

SEDUM LINEARE

SEDUM BREVIFOLIUM

SEDUM SPURIUM

SELAGINELLA

SOLEIROLIA SOLEIROLII

STREPTOCARPUS

Sensitive plant (See *Mimosa pudica*).
Sickle-thorn asparagus (See *Asparagus falcatus*).
Siderasis fuscata. A rosette of oval green leaves with velvet red hairs, purple undersides, and a white midrib. Grow in standard potting mix containing extra humus at temperatures from 60° to 70°. Water when dry and place in good light. Use in large, accessible containers. Large leaves cannot pass through a narrow opening.

Silk oak (See *Grevillea robusta*).
Silver lace (See *Pteris quadriaurita* 'Argyraea').
Silver Pothos (See *Rhapidophora aurea*).
Sinningia pusilla (miniature gloxinia). Long-tubed lavender flowers striped with green are slipper-shaped and contrast with the small, puckered, olive green leaves. This miniature plant from Brazil grows to just 2 inches. Plant tubers in a potting mix with added humus. Gloxinias require warmth, humidity, and shade; don't allow temperature to drop below 60°. Plant in accessible spot for lifting tubers, removing dead flowers.

Snake plant (See *Sansevieria trifasciata*).
Snapweed (See *Impatiens walleriana*).
Soleirolia soleirolii, also *Helxine soleirolii* (baby's tears). Native to Corsica. Delicate creeping plants with tiny, mosslike leaves and thread-thin stems create a lush ground cover. Plants prefer standard potting mix, filtered light, high humidity, and

SPATHIPHYLLUM CANNAEFOLIUM

SPATHIPHYLLUM CANNAEFOLIUM

ample water. Need some fresh air periodically. See photo, page 76.

Spathiphyllum cannaefolium (spathe flower). Dark green, lance-shaped leaves grow on slender stalks with white flowers that resemble calla lilies. Plant in a mixture of half humus, half garden loam. Requires high humidity, frequent waterings, and good light but no direct sun. See photos, above. (Also commonly available: *S. wallisii*, *S. 'Mauna Loa'*, *S. 'Clevelandii'*; all are similar in appearance.)

Spider Plant (See *Chlorophytum comosum* 'Vittatum'.

Spike Moss (See *Selaginella*).

Spleenwort (See *Asplenium*).

Sprenger asparagus (See *Asparagus, ornamental*).

Strawberry begonia (See *Saxifraga sarmentosa*).

Strawberry geranium (See *Saxifraga sarmentosa*).

Streptocarpus (cape primrose). Large, fleshy, sometimes velvety leaves and trumpet-shaped flowers in white, pink, purple, red, and blue. Related to African violets and gloxinias and requires similar care: same loose potting mix used for African violets, even moisture, warmth, and high humidity. See photos, right, page 76.

String of hearts (See *Ceropegia woodii*).

Striped inch plant (See *Callisia elegans*).

Sundew (See *Drosera rotundifolia*).

STREPTOCARPUS 'CONSTANT NYMPH'

Sweat plant (See *Selaginella*).

Swedish ivy (See *Plectranthus*).

Sweet flag (See *Acorus gramineus variegatus*).

Sword fern (See *Nephrolepis*).

Syngonium podophyllum. Fast-growing, climbing, or creeping vine with arrow-shaped or lobed green leaves on long stalks. There are many varieties of this tropical American plant. Prefers potting mix with added humus, average indoor temperatures and humidity, and light condition varying from semi-sunny to shady. Quickly grows too large for smaller bottle gardens. See photos, below.

Table fern (See *Pteris*).

Texas privet (See *Ligustrum japonicum*).

Threadleaf false aralia (See *Dizygotheca elegantissima*).

Tolmiea menziesii (piggy-back plant, pick-a-back). Heart-shaped, apple green leaves have delicate fuzz and toothed edges. The common names come from the tiny plantlets that grow on top of older leaves. Native to the coastal ranges from northern California to Alaska, this plant prefers filtered or no sun, around a 65° temperature, standard potting mix, and average indoor humidity and moisture. See photo, page 79.

Touch-me-not (See *Impatiens walleriana*).

Tradescantia. From Central America, these plants are grown for their foliage. Frequent pruning is necessary to keep plants from being invasive. Tolerates any soil, light conditions from sunny to semi-shady, average indoor temperatures, and average waterings. Good in hanging gardens. See photo, page 79.

T. fluminensis (wandering Jew). Fast growing with a trailing habit, succulent stems. Leaves banded with white or yellow.

T. virginiana (common spiderwort, inch plant). Upright or arching, grasslike foliage.

Trailing velvet plant (See *Ruellia makoyana*).

Tripogandra multiflora. Tender, miniature wandering Jew. Freely branching creeper with olive green leaves, purple underneath. Keep in filtered light, average house temperatures; give average amounts of moisture.

Umbrella plant (See *Cyperus alternifolius*).

Velvet plant (See *Gynura aurantiaca*).

Venus fly trap (See *Dionaea muscipula*).

Victoria fern (See *Pteris*).

Vinca minor (dwarf periwinkle). Shiny, evergreen leaves on trailing, wiry stems. Requires some moisture, humidity, and shade. Plant in standard potting mix.

Viola odorata (violet). Many moisture-loving violets are suitable for a cool garden. Grow in a rich,

SYNGONIUM PODOPHYLLUM

SYNGONIUM PODOPHYLLUM

TOLMIEA MENZIESII

TRADESCANTIA

moist potting mix with some sphagnum moss added to ensure good drainage. Excessive moisture may cause stem and leaf rot. Temperatures over 70° cause plants to become leggy. Bright light is needed for plants to bloom. See photo, right.

Violet (See *Viola*).

Wandering Jew (See *Tradescantia, Zebrina pendula,* and *Tripogandra multiflora*).

Watermelon peperomia (See *Peperomia sandersii*).

Wax flower (See *Hoya carnosa*).

Waxleaf privet (See *Ligustrum japonicum*).

Wax plant (See *Hoya carnosa*).

Wood fern (See *Dryopteris erythrosora*).

Yew pine (See *Podocarpus macrophyllus maki*).

Zebrina pendula (wandering Jew). A trailing plant, similar to *Tradescantia fluminensis,* which shares its common name. Not as hardy as *Tradescantia,* this native of tropical Mexico and Central America has purplish oval leaves and fleshy stems; there are many variegated forms. Climbs and trails in shade but needs strong light for colorful leaves. Grows in standard potting mix, at least 30% humidity, and ample water.

VIOLA ODORATA

Index

To find a plant description, look up plant names, listed alphabetically, in the Plant Selection Guide, pages 44-79. This index gives page numbers for general information on Terrariums and Miniature Gardens only.

PHOTOGRAPHERS: William Aplin: 24 right; 25 right; 50 top; 65 bottom right; 74; 75; 77 top right. **Glenn M. Christiansen:** 54 bottom right. **Richard Dawson:** 49 bottom; 58 top. **Richard Dunmire:** 55 top. **Alyson Smith Gonsalves:** 27 left. **Elsa Knoll:** 62 bottom. **Roy Krell:** 58 bottom left. **Ells Marugg:** 4 top; 10; 18; 19; 22; 23; 43 bottom; 44 top; 46 top, bottom left; 47; 48; 49 top left; 50 bottom right; 51 bottom; 53 top, bottom right; 54 bottom left; 55 bottom; 56 bottom right; 57 bottom left, right; 58 bottom right; 59 bottom; 60 bottom; 61 top left, right; 62 top left, right; 63; 64 top; 65 top, bottom left; 66 bottom; 67; 68; 69; 70; 71; 72 top left; 73; 76; 77 top left; 78; 79 top left, right. **Don Normark:** 28 bottom; 39; 42; 43 top left, right; 44 bottom; 46 bottom right; 49 top right; 51 top; 53 bottom left; 54 top; 56 top, bottom left; 57 top; 59 top; 61 bottom left, right; 72 bottom. **Norman A. Plate:** 32. **Pete Redpath:** 36. **John Robinson:** 66. **Lars Speyer:** 4 bottom; 9; 12; 14; 15. **Blair Stapp:** 28 top. **Betty Stoehr:** 77 bottom. **Darrow M. Watt:** 13; 21; 24 left; 25 left; 26; 27 right; 30; 31; 34; 35; 38; 40; 50 bottom left; 52; 60 top; 64 bottom; 72 top right. **Joe Williamson:** 79 bottom.

Special Consultants: Jean Lane, 19 top. Bob Nass, 4 top. Debbie Rinaldi, 23 top. Daphne Smith, 13, 27 left. Douglas Winget, 19 bottom.